*Cities
without
Suburbs*

Cities without Suburbs

Fourth Edition: A Census 2010 Perspective

David Rusk

W *Published by Woodrow Wilson Center Press, Washington, D.C.*

Distributed by The Johns Hopkins University Press, Baltimore and London

EDITORIAL OFFICES
Woodrow Wilson Center Press
Woodrow Wilson International Center for Scholars
One Woodrow Wilson Plaza
1300 Pennsylvania Avenue NW
Washington, D.C. 20004-3027
www.wilsoncenter.org

Order from
The Johns Hopkins University Press
Hampden Station
P.O. Box 50370
Baltimore, Maryland 20211
Telephone 1-800-527-5487
www.press.jhu.edu/books/

Library of Congress Cataloging-in-Publication Data

Rusk, David.
Cities without suburbs : a Census 2010 perspective / David Rusk. -- Fourth edition.
pages cm
Includes index.
ISBN 978-1-938027-03-1 -- ISBN 978-1-938027-04-8 1. Urban policy--United States. 2.
Metropolitan government--United States. 3. Metropolitan areas--United States. I. Title.
HT123.R84 2013
307.760973--dc23
                                        2013011110

To Delcia,
my wife
and
partner

Contents

Boxes

Tables

Preface

This short book is written for public policy makers. Its intended audience is our new president and his administration, U.S. senators and representatives, state governors, legislators, city and county elected officials—and key staff everywhere who behind the scenes help make American government work. I also wrote the book for thoughtful and concerned citizens who are prepared to think in a different way about what has happened in and around their communities and who will spur their public officials to take decisive action.

This was the audience I targeted in the preface to the first edition of *Cities without Suburbs*. My book found another unexpected readership as well—thousands of college students for whom this short (and relatively inexpensive) book was adopted for coursework. Since its publication in April 1993, *Cities without Suburbs* has clearly had an impact on those audiences. Though hardly received on the scale of the latest best-selling novel, the original book went through seven printings, encouraging the publishers to issue revised editions in 1995 and 2003. Its themes were reviewed or discussed in several hundred magazine and newspaper articles and were increasingly cited in scholarly works. *Cities without Suburbs* also helped launch a new phase of my career. During the past two decades, I have been invited to speak and consult in more than 120 metropolitan areas, ranging in size from Sharon, Pennsylvania, to New York, New York, and covering the country from Miami, Florida, to Seattle, Washington.

If all this sounds too self-congratulatory, I must acknowledge the tremendous difference between the world of opinion and the world of decision. Has *Cities without Suburbs* really changed anything anywhere? Is life better in any communities in this country as a result of my efforts?

In terms of the world of opinion, definitely. During these two decades, the metropolitan perspective has been widely embraced. Through my writing and speaking; through the activities of my comrades-in-arms, john powell (formerly at Ohio State University's

Kirwan Institute for the Study of Race and Ethnicity and now at the University of California, Berkeley's Haas Center for Diversity and Inclusion) and Myron Orfield (at the University of Minnesota's Institute on Race and Poverty); and through the work of Manuel Pastor (at the University of Southern California's Program for Environmental and Regional Equity), Xavier de Souza Briggs (at the Massachusetts Institute of Technology), Angela Glover Blackwell (at PolicyLink), Bruce Katz (at the Brookings Institution), and many others, we have created (or revived) what has been called the "regionalism movement." (Indeed, one reviewer has tagged *Cities without Suburbs* as "the bible of the regionalism movement.")

In terms of the world of decision (that is, public policy), however, the most hopeful answer is "just barely." Some cities, such as Fort Wayne, Memphis, and Springfield, Ohio, have been moved to reinvigorate their annexation policies. A handful of others (Augusta, Louisville, and Kansas City, Kansas) have successfully consolidated with their counties. To discourage suburban sprawl and urban disinvestment, some states, such as Maryland and Tennessee, have adopted more stringent growth management laws. A growing list of more than 400 communities (including Baltimore) has enacted inclusionary zoning laws that mandate integrating modest proportions of low-income housing within new, larger middle-class housing developments. The U.S. Department of Housing and Urban Development (HUD) is tearing down high-density "warehouses" for the poor and replacing them with mixed-income "urban villages." HUD has joined with the U.S. Department of Transportation and the U.S. Environmental Protection Agency to launch the Sustainable Communities Initiative. In 2008, the New Jersey legislature enacted the most important fair-share housing legislation in the nation in the past two decades as well as a sweeping reform of state aid for the education of low-income children. For these examples, my contribution ranged from being only a marginal part of the background noise to playing a direct and decisive role.

Why a new *Cities without Suburbs*? A lesser reason is that this new book is enriched now by two decades of experience in the field and by my greater familiarity with the growing body of scholarly work. But the larger reason is that Census 2010 and the multiyear American Community Survey now provide a penetrating new scan of urban America's demographic, social, and economic trends down to the neighborhood level.

Two decades later, do the lessons about urban America I proposed in the original *Cities without Suburbs* still hold up? To highlight what may be different emerging trends, many of the book's tables summarize results not just from 1950 to 2010, but also results during the 2000s. However, to jump to the end of the story (and only slightly modify the French), "the more things change, the more they remain (almost) the same."

The foundation of this book, first and foremost, is my practical experience—political and managerial—as mayor of Albuquerque from 1977 to 1981. Four years as chief executive of the largest city in New Mexico may not, in some readers' opinion, qualify me as an expert on America's cities. However, Albuquerque is a bigger city— and its city hall runs a bigger city government—than such literally big-league cities as Atlanta, Buffalo, Cincinnati, Cleveland, Miami, Minneapolis (and St. Paul), New Orleans, Oakland, Pittsburgh, and St. Louis. Within 10 or 20 years at most, Albuquerque's population will surpass that of the cities of Baltimore, Milwaukee, and perhaps even Detroit.

All this is occurring because, as a "core city," Albuquerque is growing, and the others are shrinking! The reason an Albuquerque grows and a Baltimore, Cleveland, or St. Louis shrinks—what I call a city's "elasticity"—is essential for understanding the relative health of core cities across the nation today.

Other practical career experiences shape this book. Before becoming mayor, I spent three years as a state legislator in New Mexico and five years as a civil rights and antipoverty worker with the Washington Urban League. Also valuable was my federal government experience as the U.S. Manpower Administration's legislative services chief.

Importantly, this book is the product of painstaking, hands-on research. My wife, Delcia, and I have passed endless days unearthing data from old census publications. My long backward look over the past six decades forced us to laboriously copy and then to enter more than 750,000 pieces of information into the database of our personal computer. Beyond census data, for some communities, I have searched out property assessment reports, copied down key data from school-by-school report cards on the Internet, and analyzed realtors' and homebuilders' reports on home sales prices. With gratitude, I have eagerly seized on other analysts' cataloguing of urban phenomena from David Miller's Metropolitan Power Diffusion Index to Richard Florida's Creativity Index to Myron Orfield's visually provocative five-color maps.

I originally decided to write *Cities without Suburbs* as an act of hope and faith. I believe that the problem this book addresses—the "urban problem"—is the toughest issue in American society. It goes right to the heart of the deep-rooted fears about race and social class that have had so much to do with shaping urban America today.

Yet two decades' active involvement in more than 120 communities has both sharpened my understanding of this challenge and sustained my optimism. The issue is not so much urban poverty overall as *highly concentrated* urban poverty in certain central cities and older suburbs, in poverty-impacted neighborhoods, and among Blacks and Hispanics (as contrasted with non-Hispanic Whites). In America in 2010, there were 20.4 million poor Whites compared with 10.1 million poor Blacks and 12.3 million poor Hispanics. In a typical metropolitan area, however, where 84 percent of all poor people lived, three out of four poor Whites lived in middle-class neighborhoods scattered widely across the whole region; by contrast, three out of four poor Blacks and one out of two poor Hispanics lived in poverty-impacted inner-city and inner-suburb neighborhoods.

Inner-city and (increasingly) inner-suburb poverty appears insurmountable because of this very high degree of concentration. Yet even as we claw our way back out of the deepest economic crisis since the Great Depression, America is not some Third World country where the poor are many and the middle class are few. Of every 100 residents of America's metropolitan areas, about 7 are poor and White—and they are mostly integrated into middle-class society. Of every 100 residents, only about 7 are poor and Black or Hispanic—but they are much more isolated from the middle-class mainstream. Middle-class America has the capacity to absorb poor Blacks and Hispanics as it already absorbs most poor Whites. What is lacking too often is not the resources but the political will.

Nevertheless, seen in this regional context, the manageable scale of the problem is one source of my optimism. And I have met and worked with so many concerned and engaged citizens and organizations in the hundred communities that I have visited that I have confidence that the political will to change can be generated as well.

My colleague john powell has said that "if racism were to vanish overnight in America, little would change, because the economic incentives of the current system are so powerful for those who now benefit." What these two decades have taught me most is that building political coalitions to achieve fundamental reforms in the rules of the game is hard, time-consuming work.

As Winston Churchill once commented, "at the end of the day, the American people will do the right thing—after they have exhausted all other alternatives." I have faith that our political debates, as

Abraham Lincoln testified in his first inaugural address, will be "again touched, as surely they will be, by the angels of our better nature." The policy debate must be framed not as a choice between conservative and liberal philosophies, but as a choice between policies that work and policies that do not work. The purpose of *Cities without Suburbs* is to point out what works.

Acknowledgments

I must begin by thanking all the thousands of public officials, urban professionals, citizen activists, college professors, and their students who have read the first three editions of *Cities without Suburbs*. Without your interest there would be no Census 2010 edition, and many have made comments and suggestions that have contributed to this being, I believe, a much better book than its predecessors.

I must also express my gratitude to the many committed community leaders I have met in the more than 350 organizations that have sponsored my visits to more than 120 communities during the two past decades. They have been my mentors in an ever-fascinating postgraduate seminar on urban America. Their insights and experiences enrich this book.

In a more direct sense, this book would not have been possible without the support of two extraordinary institutions. The first is the Woodrow Wilson International Center for Scholars, which invited me to serve as a guest scholar first in summer 1992, again in summer 2002, and most recently in summer 2011 to complete the research and writing of *Cities without Suburbs*. In particular, I received invaluable assistance from my excellent research associates, Daniel Green (1992), Ricky Moore (2002), and Ashley Engel (2011), a very talented, budding urban affairs professional who has contributed two essays to this volume. I am particularly grateful to Joseph Brinley, head of the Wilson Center Press, and to my editors, Linda Stringer and Laura Glassman of Publications Professionals LLC, for their wise guidance and support.

The second institution is the U.S. Bureau of the Census. In my experience, our Census Bureau provides an understanding of our nation's demographic, social, and economic trends that is unmatched internationally. Moreover, with the support of its ever-helpful professional staff, I have found it a pleasure through the years to be able to browse among the stacks of the Census Bureau Library and pull off the shelf any census publication going back to 1790 or, more recently, to download the voluminous materials now available online.

Throughout these two decades my wife, Delcia, has been my business manager, data entry assistant, travel companion, and best critic, both my rudder and my even keel. The professional life on which this book is based would have been impossible without her love and support.

Introduction: Framing the Issue

Not so very long ago, Grand Rapids, Michigan, and Charlotte, North Carolina, were quite similar cities. On key demographic and economic indicators, they matched up quite well.[1]

In 1950, both had about the same number of residents: Charlotte 134,042 and Grand Rapids 176,525.

Within its city limits, Charlotte embraced a little more territory (30.0 square miles) than did Grand Rapids (23.4 square miles).

In 1950, residents of both cities had somewhat higher incomes than their suburban neighbors—Grand Rapids more than 2 percent higher, Charlotte more than 5 percent higher.[2]

Their regional economies were also very similar, employing about the same proportion of workers in manufacturing and agriculture.

The biggest difference was purely cosmetic. The Grand Rapids area was almost 98 percent White, whereas the Charlotte area was 25 percent Black.[3]

In short, if not exactly twin cities, in 1950 Grand Rapids and Charlotte were at least first cousins. Six decades later, the differences between the two cities were so great that Grand Rapids and Charlotte hardly seemed to be members of the same species.

By 2010, at 731,424 residents (more than five times its 1950 population), Charlotte had become the 17th most populous city in the United States. By contrast, since 1950, the population of Grand Rapids had grown just 6 percent to 188,040, making it only the 111th most populous city in the country (dropping from 56th place in 1950).

Charlotte's city limits had exploded. By 2010, Charlotte covered 297.7 square miles (almost 10 times its area in 1950). Although Grand Rapids almost doubled its municipal territory to 44.4 square miles in the 1960s, its city limits had been frozen ever since.

Remember how both cities' average family was economically better off than its average suburban neighbor in 1950? By 2010, Grand Rapids residents' incomes had dropped 22 percent below suburban levels, whereas Charlotte residents' incomes were still equal to (or substantially above) suburban levels.[4]

Over these six decades, both regions experienced dramatic economic transformation, including major declines in industrial employment (which hit the Charlotte area harder than the Grand Rapids area).[5] Yet Charlotte had literally become a "big league" city (home to the National Football League's Carolina Panthers and the National Basketball Association's Charlotte Bobcats), whereas Grand Rapids remained firmly branded as "minor league."

Certainly, over these six decades the Charlotte region has grown more dramatically than has the greater Grand Rapids region. Adjusting the one-county Charlotte metropolitan area of 1950 retroactively to its six-county geography in 2010, one finds that the Charlotte area's population more than tripled in these six decades. After making a similar adjustment, one finds that the greater Grand Rapids area's population only doubled.[6]

Yet the 3-to-2 advantage in regional rates of population growth hardly explains Charlotte's almost 70-to-1 advantage over Grand Rapids in municipal population growth rate. The explanation clearly lies in Charlotte's almost sevenfold increase in geographic size over Grand Rapids.

As is developed in subsequent chapters, Charlotte is a very "elastic" city. In the post–World War II Age of Sprawl, as the Charlotte region has expanded ever outward, the city of Charlotte has been able to expand its boundaries dramatically to capture a great deal of suburban-style development. By contrast, after an initial two decades of modest expansion, the city boundaries of Grand Rapids have been frozen from the late 1960s onward; almost all new development has occurred in independent suburbs outside its city limits. Grand Rapids is an "inelastic" city.

As is shown in this book, a core city's relative elasticity or inelasticity has a profound impact on its population growth, its racial and ethnic makeup, city dwellers' income and poverty levels compared to suburban levels, and a city's fiscal health (as measured by its municipal bond rating).

A core city's relative elasticity even has some implications for its region's economic growth, particularly because most inelastic cities are surrounded by myriad incorporated "little boxes" suburbs—a highly fragmented environment that promotes internecine warfare and impedes unified regional action. Elastic cities exist within "Big Box" regions where counterproductive, interjurisdictional rivalries are lessened and collaborative initiatives are less difficult to achieve.

Prior to the emergence of the regionalism movement, debate over urban policy focused typically on only a handful of America's largest core cities. Such cities typified America's "urban problem": intense racial and economic segregation that created an underclass that, in turn, spawned physically decaying, revenue-strapped, poverty-impacted, crime-ridden "inner cities." These inner cities were isolated from their "outer cities"—wealthier, growing, still largely White suburbs.

What these two decades have reemphasized since the first edition of *Cities without Suburbs* (1993) is that all suburbs are not the same. Many "First Suburbs" (that is, the suburbs usually developed first outside central cities) have become highly diverse—racially, ethnically, and economically. Many embody the vision of what many Americans say we want to be as a nation. But such communities are very fragile and at risk. Their very diversity may be only temporary, and unchanged "rules of the game" promote racial and economic resegregation.

Rather than focus just on the usual targets of "urban policy," this book looks at all urban areas and examines in detail 137 urban areas with populations of 350,000 or more. Also, it focuses on entire metropolitan areas—cities and suburbs.

This broader perspective will yield, I hope, greater clarity about what has been happening in urban America. Lessons can be learned from many urban areas that are rarely analyzed. Bad lessons can be drawn from areas such as Harrisburg and Syracuse, and success stories may be learned, for example, from Madison and my own Albuquerque.[7]

In highly segregated metro areas—no matter how wealthy areawide—concentrated poverty, joblessness, and crime compound each other; as a result, almost without exception, their core cities are failing. In more integrated metro areas—even when poorer areawide—poverty, dependency, and crime lack a certain critical mass; their core cities are succeeding.

In about half the country's large metro areas—those with inelastic cities—social and economic inequities are severe. In the other half, however, good timing, good luck, and good public policy resulting in elastic cities have combined to create more successful communities for Whites, Blacks, and Hispanics alike.

From my research on all 383 metropolitan areas in the United States, I have derived 26 lessons about what has been happening in urban America since World War II. The statistical analysis typically begins with the 1950 census and ends with the 2010 census. The first four lessons stated in Chapter 1 ("Lessons from Urban America") are supported by data drawn from all 383 metropolitan areas within the country. Thereafter, in an effort to communicate in as clear and jargon-free a manner as possible, I illustrate the remaining 22 lessons by contrasting eight specific pairs of metropolitan areas: Charlotte and Grand Rapids, Houston and Detroit, Columbus and Cleveland, Nashville and Louisville, Indianapolis and Milwaukee, Albuquerque and Syracuse, Madison and Harrisburg, and Raleigh and Richmond. These lessons, however, were originally framed by analyzing trends in 137 metropolitan areas with more than 350,000 inhabitants.

In Chapter 2 ("Characteristics of Metropolitan Areas"), I divide these 137 larger metropolitan areas into five broad categories. For each of these broad categories, I then restate lessons introduced in Chapter 1.

Unlike in the original edition of *Cities without Suburbs*, in Chapter 3 ("Strategies for Stretching Cities") of this Census 2010 edition, I do not focus as much on policies that lead formally to more unified local governance, such as municipal annexation powers and city–county consolidation. Altering local political boundaries is legally impossible throughout New England, New York, New Jersey, and Pennsylvania and pragmatically impossible around many older core cities, particularly in much of the Midwest.

As a consequence, I devote increased attention to what one critic called "elasticity mimics"—that is, regional growth management policies, regional fair-share housing policies (inclusionary zoning), and regional tax-base-sharing policies.[8] Adopting these recommendations (thereby changing the rules of the game) can profoundly improve the long-term outlook for core cities and their regions.

Finally, Chapter 4 restates my conclusions and offers some final observations.

This Census 2010 edition benefits from an invaluable, postpublication insight regarding the original *Cities without Suburbs*: what an author thinks he writes may not be what some readers read. So let me be clear about what are (and are not) the principal themes of this edition of *Cities without Suburbs*:

1) The book is primarily an explanation of why, in the Age of Sprawl, some core cities, as municipalities, are relatively healthy and growing and others are relatively troubled and declining.

2) The book argues that "Big Box" regions, with their steadily expanding core cities and larger (often countywide) school districts, implicitly facilitate greater racial and economic in-

tegration, whereas "little boxes" regions (where the core city and school system are trapped within inflexible boundaries, surrounded by myriad independent suburbs and school districts) are characterized by greater racial and economic segregation.

3) This book does not (nor did it ever originally intend to) propose a theory of economic development, though I certainly contend that both cities and suburbs are integral components of regional economies. Yet evidence indicates that intense fragmentation of local government within a region has adverse impacts on the rate of economic growth.

I often told Albuquerque audiences that New Mexico is one of the few places where a Puccini, a Pulaski, and a Goldstein could all be called Anglo. Throughout the book, when I refer to *White*, I mean Anglo—that is, non-Hispanic Whites. And contrary to commonly accepted editorial style, I refer to Whites, Blacks, and Hispanics with coequal capital letters. I do not mean to slight either the problems or achievements of urban Asians and Native Americans by not focusing on them. However, my analysis indicates that social and political attitudes in America revolve around only Whites, Blacks, and Hispanics with sufficient force and magnitude to influence patterns of urban growth.

Notes

1.   The underlying premises and assertions made in the Grand Rapids/ Charlotte comparison were originally published in David Rusk, "Changing The 'Rules of the Game': Tools to Revive Michigan's Fractured Metropolitan Regions," *Journal of Law in Society* 13, no. 1 (2011): 197–266.

2.   At a median family income of $3,660, Grand Rapids was 102 percent of the metropolitan median family income ($3,594), while Charlotte's median family income ($3,346) was 105 percent of the metropolitan median ($3,180) in 1949. Because a city's statistics are part of the metropolitan statistics, the city-to-suburb percentage would be greater than the city-to-metropolitan area percentage.

3.   In the 1950 census, the official terminology was nonwhite, a classification that also included Asians and American Indians (both of which were negligible presences in the Grand Rapids and Charlotte areas at mid-20th century).

4.   In 2009, the median family income ($46,779) in Grand Rapids was only 78 percent of the metropolitan area's median family income ($59,999), while Charlotte had maintained virtual parity (city median of $63,516 compared with a metropolitan median of $64,276). By another measure—per capita in-

come (which was not tabulated by the U.S. Census Bureau until the 1980 census)—in 2009, Charlotte city residents' per capita income ($31,839) was 119 percent of suburban per capita income ($26,792), while Grand Rapids city residents' per capita income ($20,196) was 79 percent of suburban per capita income ($25,569).

5.   According to the U.S. Bureau of Economic Analysis online Regional Economic Accounts, despite West Michigan's image as a "smokestack economy" with a diversified industrial base, by 2009, factory jobs declined less as a proportion of the regional labor force in West Michigan (41 percent to 15 percent) than in the Charlotte region (38 percent to 7 percent). The Charlotte area's textile industries were almost totally wiped out.

6.   Between 1950 and 2010, the combined population of the seven counties that formed Charlotte–Gastonia–Rock Hill, NC–SC, metropolitan statistical area (MSA) by the latter date grew from 512,082 to 1,758,038 persons. Although the Grand Rapids–Wyoming, MI, MSA was officially defined as only Kent, Barry, Ionia, and Newaygo counties for 2010, the federal definition of the Grand Rapids–Muskegon–Holland, MI, Combined Statistical Area added Muskegon, Ottawa, and Allegan counties, each of which has been included in past definitions of the Grand Rapids metropolitan area by the federal Office of Management and Budget. This book has treated this seven-county area as the West Michigan region. Its combined population grew from 616,989 in 1950 to 1,323,598 in 2010.

7.   In general, I do not identify cities by state except to make a rhetorical point. Readers can refer to Table 2.1 for identification of the 137 cities with their states. However, I do distinguish between Springfield, Massachusetts, and Springfield, Missouri, and between Wilmington, Delaware, and Wilmington, North Carolina.

8.   These policies are discussed at great length in my book *Inside Game/Outside Game: Winning Strategies for Saving Urban America* (Washington, DC: Brookings Institution Press, 1999).

Chapter 1

Lessons from Urban America

Despite the romance of the frontier, the true land of opportunity in America for more than 150 years has been the cities. From farms and foreign lands, migrants and immigrants flocked into the cities, seeking better schools, better jobs, and better health care—in short, a better life. What lessons can be drawn from a broad look at what has been happening in urban America over the past 60 years?

Lesson 1: The Real City Is the Total Metropolitan Area—City and Suburb

At the end of World War II, urban America was still the inner cities. Hardly any outer cities existed. The suburban movement was just starting. The country's biggest cities were booming and bursting at the seams. Drawn by the war industries, millions had left farms and small towns to pack into the cities.

In 1950, almost 70 percent of the population of 168 metropolitan areas lived in 193 central cities. (For an explanation of Census Bureau terms, see Box 1.1.) City residents attended the same city school system. They used the city parks and libraries. They rode city buses, streetcars, and subways to blue- and white-collar jobs within the city or, occasionally, in nearby suburbs. They fought for control of the same city hall. Although there were often fierce conflicts among ethnic and racial groups, common public institutions were unifying forces (except in the segregated South).

Today the situation is reversed. By 2010, almost 68 percent of the population of 383 metropolitan areas lived in suburbs.[1] Equally as important, suburbs no longer simply served as bedroom communities for workers with city-based jobs. By 2010, a majority of jobs in metro areas were located in suburbs as well.[2]

Box 1.1 What Is a Metropolitan Area?

According to the U.S. Bureau of the Census, a *metropolitan area* (metropolitan statistical area, MSA, or metro area) is "a core area containing a substantial population nucleus, together with adjacent communities having a high degree of economic and social integration with that core."[a] In short, a metro area is a city and its suburbs.

Each metro area must include a "central city" that, with contiguous, densely settled territory, constitutes a Census Bureau–defined urbanized area of at least 50,000 people. If the largest city has fewer than 50,000 people, the area must have a total population of at least 100,000.

In 1910, the Census Bureau first introduced *metropolitan districts*. Since then, it has used many different methodologies to define metro areas, but by 1950 it had settled on using entire counties as the building blocks of metro areas (except, until Census 2010, in New England). Counties outside of the "central county" in which the central city is located are added on the basis of workers' commuting patterns into the central city or the central county.

In recent decades, the Census Bureau has recognized additional central cities beyond the historic focal points of many metro areas (and has restyled all as "principal cities"). Now there are 667 central cities in 348 metro areas. A metro area's title may include up to three central cities, such as Tampa–St. Petersburg–Clearwater, FL MSA. Eleven of the largest MSAs are subdivided into two or more "metropolitan divisions" (29 in all).

In this book the basic unit of analysis is an MSA or metropolitan division.[b] (I have further subdivided the official New York City, NY–NJ metropolitan division into its more traditional New York City plus three suburban New York counties, Bergen-Passaic (Paterson), NJ and Jersey City, NJ.

In metro areas of more than one central city, only the first named city is treated as the central city (for example, Tampa for Tampa–St. Petersburg–Clearwater, FL), except for Norfolk, VA.

All metro areas are analyzed as they were defined for Census 2010. A metro area's population in 1950 includes the populations in 1950 of all counties considered part of the metro area in 2010 rather than of those entities that defined the metro area under 1950 conditions.

a. See, for example, the definition on the Census Bureau's website at http://www.census.gov/population/metro/about/.

b. In 2003, the Census Bureau (or more accurately, the federal Office of Management and Budget) created the new category of micropolitan statistical areas, which numbered 574 by Census 2010. I have not analyzed trends in such small-scale microregions.

The traditional city no longer is "the place to be" for families seeking a better life. In fact, housing, jobs, schools, and services are worse in many central cities than they are in the neighboring suburbs. Any attack on urban social and economic problems must treat suburb and city as indivisible parts of a whole.

Lesson 2: Most of America's Blacks, Hispanics, and Asians Live in Metro Areas

Sixty years ago, the country's 15 million Blacks were still substantially rural and southern, although the Great Migration into cities north and south had been under way since about 1910 and accelerated during World War II. Similarly, many of the country's Hispanics were scattered in small towns and cities located largely throughout the Southwest. Asian Americans, always an urban people, were heavily concentrated in West Coast cities.

In 1950, America's population was about 86 percent to 87 percent White and 13 percent to 14 percent minority (including Native Americans).[3] Sixty years later America is 36 percent minority, and almost 90 percent of all minorities live in metropolitan areas. In fact, a majority of all Blacks, Hispanics, and Asians live in just 22 metro areas.[4]

Today, minorities as well as opportunity are concentrated in metro areas. Social and economic equality can be achieved only through what happens in metro areas.

Lesson 3: Since World War II, Most Urban Growth Has Been Low Density, Suburban Style

The 1950 census was the high-water mark for most of America's big cities. Of the 12 largest cities, 9 (all except New York, Los Angeles, and San Francisco) hit their 20th-century population peaks in the 1950 census.

Thereafter, Washington, Wall Street, Detroit, Hollywood, and Madison Avenue made middle-class families an offer they could not refuse: the American Dream. Sustained economic growth, cheap home mortgages, affordable automobiles, and federally subsidized highways—all touted on screens big and small—made that dream house with its own yard, quiet neighborhood, local school, and nearby shopping possible for millions of families. Compared with staying put in many city neighborhoods, suburbia was a bargain. Urban America became Suburban America.

Everyone knows this. What is not always recognized is how universal this pattern has been in postwar America.

The Census Bureau defines "urbanized areas" as the urbanized core of metropolitan areas: the central city and its contiguous, built-up suburbs. Let's focus briefly on urbanized areas as another way to measure the march of suburbanization.

In 1950, 69 million people lived in 157 urbanized areas that covered 12,715 square miles. By 2010, those same 157 urbanized areas contained 169 million residents in 60,558 square miles of developed land—well over double the population but occupying almost five times as much land. Although many cities had expanded their boundaries, 78 percent of the newly developed land and almost 82 percent of the added population were located in suburbs outside central cities.

Population density measures how many people live in a given square mile. Suburbanization cut the population density of these 157 urbanized areas almost in half from 5,391 persons per square mile in 1950 to 2,795 persons per square mile in 2010. In only 10 of the 157 urbanized areas did population density increase. All 10 began the postwar period far below the average density, and 8 experienced substantial Hispanic immigration.[5]

Within core cities, population density declined as well. In 1950, for example, 40 cities had densities of 10,000 or more persons per square mile. Over the next 60 years, all of these cities except New York City and San Francisco lost density. By 2010, only 22 cities had densities of 10,000 or more persons per square mile.

Nine cities—seven of them centers of Hispanic immigration—had joined the high-density list.[6] Miami and Miami Beach, for example, were historic focal points of Cuban, Caribbean, and Central American immigration; Hispanics were 68 percent and 49 percent, respectively, of their residents by 2010.

The Pacific Rim's Ellis Island was the greater Los Angeles area, as Hispanic and Asian immigrants filled up Southern California. For example, Hispanic immigration tripled Santa Ana's density to almost 12,000 residents per square mile.

Immigration also focused on the greater New York area, the traditional port of entry (see Box 1.2). By 2010, Hispanic and Asian immigrants had lifted New York City to 8,175,133 residents (its highest population ever). Immigrants also kept Paterson, Elizabeth, New Brunswick, Perth Amboy, and Bayonne, New Jersey, filled to record levels.

In short, the only cities in America that swam against the sub-urban stream were cities swimming with the immigrant stream. A certain natural clustering of new immigrants, large families (including extended families), low incomes, and a degree of anti-Hispanic or anti-Asian discrimination in neighboring communities combined to pack immigrants into port-of-entry cities. Everywhere else, most middle-class White Americans for the past 60 years have chosen to raise young families in low-density subdivisions rather than high-density city neighborhoods.

Lesson 4: For a City's Population to Grow, the City Must Be Elastic

Think of a city as a map drawn on a rubber sheet. If a great deal of vacant land is within existing city limits, that city's population density is low. In effect, the rubber sheet map is slack. The city has room for new population growth by filling in undeveloped land. Facing growth opportunities, the city is still elastic within its boundaries because it can "infill" undeveloped land.

In contrast, what if the city is already densely populated with little or no vacant land to develop? Its rubber sheet map is stretched taut within its existing boundaries.

Most high-density cities do not become denser. Typically, a high-density city's growth strategy is to expand its boundaries. It must stretch the edges of its rubber sheet map to take in new territory. It must become more elastic outward rather than upward.

The most common method by which a city acquires new territory is annexation. Sometimes, a city annexes undeveloped land. Often, annexation brings in relatively new, unincorporated subdivisions and commercial areas.

Stretching the edges of the municipal map often creates tension—outside resistance, which is always from those to be annexed, and inside resistance, sometimes from a city's current residents. Annexation is not always easy.

How much did cities use each mechanism—filling in vacant land and annexing additional territory? Only about 25 percent of all cities actually increased their densities.[7] For many other cities, however, infill development was combined with boundary expansion (which often tended to mask the degree of infill development).

Boundary expansion contributed most to municipal elasticity. Between 1950 and 2010, over three-quarters of 684 central cities

Box 1.2 New York City, 1790–2010

My analysis focuses on different cities' elasticity amid metro growth over the past 60 years, but all cities were elastic in their youth. New York City serves as a historical microcosm for urban development patterns.

In 1790, the city of New York, located on the tip of Manhattan Island, was the country's largest city, surpassing Philadelphia, Boston, and Baltimore. It had 33,131 residents. Barely 16,000 people were scattered in villages and farms in the surrounding counties (about 50 people per square mile).

By 1890, the city of New York had packed 1.4 million residents onto Manhattan Island (New York County). Linked to the city of New York by the Brooklyn Bridge, the city of Brooklyn in Kings County was the Phoenix of the 19th century, increasing its population 20-fold between 1840 and 1890. The other surrounding counties (Bronx, Queens, and Richmond), however, were still relatively lightly populated.

In 1897, New York's state legislature created the modern New York City by converting the five counties into boroughs of a new city and abolishing all existing municipal governments, including the city of Brooklyn, the nation's seventh most populous city. This legislative act, approved over fierce lobbying opposition from wealthy suburbanites in Brooklyn, created the world's largest city (3.4 million in 1900) and the country's first metropolitan government.

Packed with new European immigrants, the old city of New York (Manhattan) had been approaching its capacity. Manhattan would still grow another 23 percent in population, but would peak by 1910. Consolidation made the city of New York elastic again, above all through the acquisition of more than 200 square miles of lightly settled land in the Bronx, Queens, and Staten Island.

For the next 50 years, much of New York City's "suburban" growth occurred within its own city limits. Brooklyn grew another 135 percent to its 1950 peak population of 2.7 million. The Bronx grew 625 percent (to 1.5 million) before flattening out after 1950. Queens grew 1,200 percent, reaching 2 million by 1970. Decade by decade, Staten Island's farms gave way to subdivisions. These earlier suburbs may have been subway-and-trolley suburbs rather than the automobile-based suburbs of the postwar decades, but they were suburbs all the same.

During the past three decades, however, accelerated immigration from Asia and Latin America lifted the populations of Queens,

Staten Island, and New York City as a whole (8,175,133) to all-time highs. Manhattan Island, the original "central city," however, had lost 32 percent from its 1910 peak population.

In 1910, when the Census Bureau conceived of metropolitan districts, it designated New York City as the hub of a region including northern New Jersey (Newark and Jersey City) and Westchester County. New York City constituted over 80 percent of the population of this region. By 1950, New York City still had 61 percent of the region's population.

Thereafter, the suburban movement exploded beyond New York's city limits. Between 1950 and 1960, Nassau and Suffolk Counties doubled to 2 million people. By 2010, Fairfield County, Connecticut, has almost also doubled to 917,000, drawing off many of Manhattan's richest executives and corporate headquarters. Commuting patterns extended the greater New York area far down into central New Jersey, where the population tripled.

For five decades, while New York City was largely *its own suburbs*, it was one of America's most successful urban communities. New York City's schools, hospitals, and city services were among the best. With all of its warts, New York City was a great magnet for those seeking a better life—and it largely delivered!

But 1950 was the watershed. From 1900 to 1950, New York City captured over 50 percent of its suburban growth; after 1950, thanks to the immigrant wave of the past two decades, the city has barely broken even. By 2010, New York City accounted for 37 percent of its regional population.[a]

When it was truly a metro government, New York City was enormously successful. When it slipped into being the central city of a metropolitan region expanding far beyond its borders, its serious social and fiscal problems began.

How elusive regional solutions are for this massive 22 million-resident, 11,674-square-mile megaregion reaching into four states is well documented in an excellent book, *Regionalism and Realism*, by Richard Nathan and Gerald Benjamin.[b] Their perceptive analysis also illustrates how difficult it is for state and local government leaders to think—and act—outside the "boxes."

a. In 2010, the population of the New York–Newark–Bridgeport, NY–NJ–CT–PA combined statistical area was 22,051,453.

b. Richard Nathan and Gerald Benjamin, *Regionalism and Realism* (Washington, DC: Brookings Institution Press, 2001).

expanded their boundaries by 10 percent or more.[8] The municipal expansion champion was Anchorage. By absorbing its entire surrounding borough, the city of Anchorage grew from 12.5 square miles to 1,697.7 square miles (13,482 percent)! Overall, the 684 central cities expanded from 11,002 square miles to 36,058 square miles (228 percent, or 217 percent if Anchorage's massive land grab is discounted). That is equivalent to annexing the whole state of West Virginia or two dozen Rhode Islands.

On the threshold of the era of the suburban lifestyle, the cities with the greatest elasticity had both vacant city land to develop *and* the political and legal tools to annex new territory. These I call "elastic" cities. At the other end of the spectrum were the "inelastic" cities—typically, older cities already built out at higher-than-average densities and, for a variety of reasons, unable or unwilling to expand their city limits.

This concept of a city's elasticity is the central idea of this book. Why have some cities been elastic and others not? What are the demographic, economic, social, and fiscal consequences of relative elasticity? If being an elastic city is essential to economic, social, and fiscal health, what can be done to make inelastic cities elastic again or, at least, to institute policies for them to benefit as if they were elastic?

* * *

Summary data for all 383 metro areas support the first four lessons I have presented. The succeeding lessons are based on analysis of 137 large metro areas but in this chapter are illustrated by contrasting specific metro areas that I have paired: Houston–Detroit, Columbus–Cleveland, Nashville–Louisville, Indianapolis–Milwaukee, Albuquerque–Syracuse, Madison–Harrisburg, Raleigh–Richmond, and (added for the 2010 edition) Charlotte–Grand Rapids. At first glance, several of the metro areas paired may seem to have nothing in common. All pairs (except Charlotte–Grand Rapids), however, were matched in terms of two key characteristics in the first edition of *Cities without Suburbs*.

First, from 1950 to 1990, the metro areas in each pair had to house roughly equivalent numbers of new-home occupants (Table 1.1). Because household sizes have fallen throughout America (except in cities with recent immigration), any additional population must be accommodated by building new housing, typically in new subdivisions. For an elastic area (Houston or Columbus, for example) new-home occupants are equivalent to net metro population growth.

Table 1.1
Each Pair of Metro Areas Had about the
Same Number of New-Home Occupants, 1950–2010

Metro area	New-home occupants	
	1950–1990 (MSA as defined for 1990 census)	1950–2010 (MSA as defined for 2010 census)
Houston	2,400,986	4,875,960
Detroit	1,957,962	2,287,490
Columbus	648,617	1,090,566
Cleveland	707,740	931,590
Nashville	483,118	1,032,282
Louisville	417,691	580,367
Indianapolis	522,700	999,960
Milwaukee	427,242	688,188
Albuquerque	334,904	707,773
Syracuse	251,473	617,110
Madison	197,728	345,603
Harrisburg	226,448	272,468
Raleigh	431,615	896,793
Richmond	429,830	773,175
Charlotte	n.a.	1,245,956
Grand Rapids	n.a.	716,369

Note: n.a. = not applicable.

For an inelastic area, however, new homes must be provided for newcomers to the metro area *and* for current residents moving from the city to the suburbs. For an inelastic area, net metro population growth *and the central city's net loss of population* are added together to calculate new-home occupants. (For an inelastic area, the term "new-home occupants" is identical to suburban population growth.

I have resisted, however, labeling it "suburban growth" because city and suburb potentially competed to house that population.)

The second factor used to pair up metro areas was racial composition. In 1990, the metro areas of each pair had roughly equivalent percentages of Black population (Table 1.2).

Although the metro areas in each pair were equivalent in new-home occupants and percentage of Black population, the relative elasticity of the central cities in each pair was not the same. The

TABLE 1.2
EACH PAIR OF METRO AREAS HAD ABOUT THE
SAME PERCENTAGE OF BLACKS IN THE POPULATION IN 1990

| | Percentage of Blacks in metro population | |
| | 1990 (MSA as defined for 1990 census) | 2010 (MSA as defined for 2010 census) |
Metro area		
Houston	19	17
Detroit	21	23
Columbus	12	15
Cleveland	19	20
Nashville	15	15
Louisville	13	14
Indianapolis	14	15
Milwaukee	14	16
Albuquerque	3	2
Syracuse	6	8
Madison	3	4
Harrisburg	7	10
Raleigh	25	20
Richmond	29	29
Charlotte	n.a.	24
Grand Rapids	n.a.	8

Note: n.a. = not applicable.

more elastic city is listed first; the less elastic city is listed second.[9] (For example, Houston is more elastic than Detroit.)

In the two decades since the first edition of *Cities without Suburbs*, most of these pairs of metro areas have grown farther apart, particularly in new-home population. Moreover, the Census Bureau has redefined metro areas (sometimes radically, in the cases of Raleigh, which lost its Durham–Chapel Hill portion, and Harrisburg, which lost its Lebanon portion); also, a dozen of these metro areas saw new counties added (seven in Richmond's case).

Nevertheless, I have retained the original pairings because they illustrate the consequences of relative city elasticity in often similar circumstances, such as two cities in the same state (Columbus and Cleveland), two state capitals in northern states (Madison and Harrisburg), two state capitals in adjacent southern states (Raleigh and Richmond), and two older industrial cities (Indianapolis and Milwaukee).

The Nashville–Louisville pairing is a particularly interesting study in elasticity. Originally, Nashville (made elastic by city–county consolidation in 1962) was contrasted with inelastic Louisville. However, right after Census 2000, Louisville achieved instant elasticity by consolidating with Jefferson County, which had an immediate impact on certain metrics for Census 2010 (see Box 1.3). Thus, I will show two comparisons for Louisville—the city alone through 2000 and the new Louisville–Jefferson County as of 2010.

Lesson 5: Almost All Metro Areas Have Grown

It is easy to label Detroit and Syracuse as "declining Frost Belt areas" and Houston and Albuquerque as "booming Sun Belt areas." The truth is, however, that the populations of Frost Belt areas as well as Sun Belt areas grew as total metropolitan areas. In fact, the populations of most metropolitan areas grew over the past six decades.

Table 1.3 presents the metro population growth of the eight pairs of metro areas. Metro areas containing elastic cities have had higher growth rates than metro areas with inelastic cities. These metro areas began at lower population levels. The inelastic areas began at much higher population levels and added to that larger base.

Growth rates, of course, are a function of how much is added to how large an initial base. Each additional resident contributes to a higher rate of growth for a smaller initial population base than for a larger initial population base. Thus, the rates of population growth among

Box 1.3 Urban Bodybuilding in Louisville–Jefferson County

In an exercise of what one noted commentator called "urban body-building," Louisville and Jefferson County consolidated on January 1, 2003.[a] It was the largest city–county consolidation in 33 years.

Local voters had twice rejected consolidation, most recently in 1983. What caused the turnaround in public sentiment for the 2000 election?

In a word, probably jealousy.

Forty years before, when Louisville's population was at its peak (390,639), Louisville competed fiercely with the city of Indianapolis (476,258), which lies some 110 miles north on Interstate 65. Louisville lorded it over Nashville (170,874) and rarely took notice of farther-off Jacksonville (201,810). Lexington (62,810) was simply the small-town home of the University of Kentucky Wildcats, archrivals of the hometown Louisville Cardinals.

Forty years later, Indianapolis, Nashville, and Jacksonville had doubled or tripled inelastic Louisville's population. With the National Football League Colts, Titans, and Jaguars, all three cities also literally achieved "big league" status, while Louisville remained a "college town."

Perhaps as galling to Louisville's pride, by 2000, even once lowly Lexington (260,512) had pushed Louisville (256,321) aside as Kentucky's biggest city.

The key for all four competitors was city–county consolidation: Nashville–Davidson (1963), Jacksonville–Duval (1968), Indianapolis–Marion (1970), and Lexington–Fayette (1973). Cosmetic rhetoric aside, a city–county consolidation is really a giant, one-time annexation by the city. By absorbing most existing suburban population (and plenty of raw land to grow on), these consolidated entities could instantly market themselves as big cities.

The Louisville–Jefferson County consolidation epitomizes a second lesson beyond the motivating power of civic jealousy: smaller

elastic areas (132 percent to 445 percent) were much higher than the growth rates among inelastic areas (24 percent to 137 percent).

Do great disparities in *rates* of population growth make a difference? Of course they do. For an area to more than double its population (Columbus, Nashville, Indianapolis, Madison); more than triple its population (Charlotte); or even increase its population about fivefold (Houston, Albuquerque, Raleigh) creates a more expansive business and community climate—even a "boomtown" psychology—than exists in an area that grows more slowly.

municipalities never join up with the merger of the county and the big city.

On the eve of consolidation in 2000, within its 62-square-mile territory, the city of Louisville contained 256,531 residents, or 36.9 percent of Jefferson County's population. However, the 93 independent smaller municipalities collectively contained another 140,197 residents, or 20.5 percent of the county's population, within their combined 56 square miles.

But with consolidation, the county's "dowry" (that is, its unincorporated area) added 294,910 residents and 269 square miles to the city—a rich dowry by any standard, even for a consolidation in which a bigger slice (the 93 smaller municipalities) was exempted from the consolidation than in any other instance.[b]

Though civic leaders touted that a consolidated Louisville–Jefferson County would instantly become the 16th-largest city in the United States, the Census Bureau deducts the population of all nonmerged municipalities from the consolidated entity. As a result, with 597,337 residents in 2010, Louisville was not the country's 16th- but its 26th-largest city (still quite some muscling up from 67th largest in its preconsolidated state).

The consolidated government is headed by a mayor and 26 council members, who are elected by district. They face many typical urban problems, but an expanded tax base and beefed-up identity are new tools to work with. These incentives might even be sufficient to lure a big league sports franchise to town.

a. Alan Ehrenhalt, "Secrets of Urban Bodybuilding," *Governing*, January 2001.

b. A number of the micromunicipalities merged with each other so that there are now 83 smaller independent municipalities with Louisville–Jefferson County. The largest is Jeffersontown (9.95 square miles and 26,595 residents in 2010). The smallest is South Park View City—just 6 acres and 7 residents in 2010!

However, the spectacular rates of population growth of some metro areas have obscured the fact that less spectacularly expanding areas added hundreds of thousands of new residents. For example, from 1950 to 2010, the Columbus metro area added 1.1 million people (net), but the Cleveland metro area added 400,000 people (net) as well. Moreover, the growth of metro Columbus and that of metro Cleveland was much closer in terms of numbers of families looking for new homes—the key to how local jurisdictions grow within the same metro area.

TABLE 1.3
ALMOST ALL METRO AREAS HAVE GROWN

	Metro population		Percentage change	
Metro area	1950	2010	1950–2010	2000s
Houston	1,090,272	5,946,800	445	26
Detroit	3,170,315	4,296,250	36	−4
Columbus	745,970	1,836,536	146	14
Cleveland	1,680,736	2,077,240	24	−3
Nashville	557,652	1,589,934	185	21
Louisville	703,199	1,283,566	83	10
Indianapolis	756,281	1,756,241	132	15
Milwaukee	1,014,211	1,555,908	53	4
Albuquerque	179,304	887,077	395	22
Syracuse	465,114	662,577	42	2
Madison	222,990	568,593	155	13
Harrisburg	317,023	549,475	73	8
Raleigh	233,697	1,130,490	384	42
Richmond	530,194	1,258,251	137	15
Charlotte	512,082	1,758,038	243	32
Grand Rapids	616,989	1,323,598	115	5

Lesson 6: Low-Density Cities Can Grow through Infill; High-Density Cities Cannot

What was the situation of our sample cities in 1950 as the American Dream picked up momentum? The average density for all 193 designated central cities in 1950 was 6,769 persons per square mile. Albuquerque,[10] Houston, and Charlotte were well below the national average (Table 1.4). They would have accommodated some additional growth within existing city limits. Raleigh, Richmond, and Madison might have had a little "room at the inn" as well. But even Grand Rapids, Indianapolis, and Nashville appeared by 1950

TABLE 1.4
Low-Density Cities Can Grow through Infill;
High-Density Cities Cannot

Central city	City density (persons per square mile), 1950	City density as a percentage of national average city density, 1950
Houston	3,726	55
Detroit	13,249	196
Columbus	9,541	141
Cleveland	12,197	180
Nashville	7,923	117
Louisville	9,251	137
Indianapolis	7,739	114
Milwaukee	12,745	188
Albuquerque	2,021	30
Syracuse	8,719	129
Madison	6,237	92
Harrisburg	14,213	210
Raleigh	5,971	88
Richmond	6,208	92
Charlotte	4,468	66
Grand Rapids	7,543	111

to have exceeded the densities associated with the emerging low-density American Dream.

Lesson 7: Elastic Cities Expand Their City Limits; Inelastic Cities Do Not

Elastic cities did not just fill up vacant areas within existing city limits. They expanded their city limits greatly (Table 1.5). Houston, Columbus, Albuquerque, Madison, and Raleigh grew through aggressive annexation of surrounding areas. After their earlier pace of annexation had slowed, Nashville and Indianapolis expanded dramatically by consolidating with their home counties, becoming unified governments.

By contrast, almost without exception, inelastic cities entered the postwar growth era locked within their existing boundaries. The city limits of Detroit and Syracuse did not budge. The city of Cleve-

TABLE 1.5
ELASTIC CITIES EXPAND THEIR CITY LIMITS; INELASTIC CITIES DO NOT

Central city	City area (square miles)		Percentage change	
	1950	2010	1950–2010	2000s
Houston	160	600	275	3
Detroit	139	139	0	0
Columbus	39	217	451	3
Cleveland	75	78	4	0
Nashville	22	475	2,060	0
Louisville (to 2000)	40	62	56	n.a.
Louisville–Jefferson County	40	325	715	424
Indianapolis	55	361	555	0
Milwaukee	50	96	92	0
Albuquerque	48	188	292	4
Syracuse	25	25	0	0
Madison	15	77	399	12
Harrisburg	6	8	29	0
Raleigh	11	143	1,199	25
Richmond	37	60	61	0
Charlotte	30	298	892	23
Grand Rapids	23.4	44	90	0

Note: n.a. = not applicable.

land added only 2 square miles, as did the city of Harrisburg. (Harrisburg's proportional growth, adding roughly one-third to its 6.3 square miles, might look significant, but the effect was minuscule within a 1,629-square-mile metro area.) After earlier annexations, Milwaukee, Richmond, and Grand Rapids are now landlocked. Louisville broke out of its jurisdictional straitjacket by consolidating with Jefferson County in January 2003.

Why were some cities so elastic and other cities very inelastic?

Lesson 8: Bad State Laws Can Hobble Cities

Constitutionally, local governments are the creatures of state government. State laws differ concerning the power they give municipalities to expand. In New England, for example, the political map has long been set in stone (in some cases, since colonial times). New England state laws do not even provide for municipal annexation. Similarly, municipal boundaries in New York, New Jersey, and Pennsylvania have been frozen for decades. Elsewhere, state statutes often attach conditions that can severely limit a municipality's practical ability to annex additional territory. Annexation may be allowed only on voluntary petition by property owners. Often an affirmative vote of affected landowners is required (or even approval by voters in the annexing municipality).

Table 1.6 summarizes a 1971 study of different cities' annexation powers and constraints. Raleigh's and Charlotte's continuous expansions were guaranteed by North Carolina's liberal annexation laws; they had the power—even the obligation—to annex urbanizing areas regardless of property owners' desires. Texas also allowed cities such as Houston to annex unincorporated areas by unilateral council action. Albuquerque's annexations had to be unanimously approved by affected property owners, but the economics of city water and sewer services motivated large land developers to seek annexation, and the city had the further power under New Mexico law to veto the incorporation of any other public body (including special water and sewer districts) within 5 miles of its boundaries.

Pennsylvania, however, had no annexation laws; Harrisburg's expansion depended on negotiating mergers with surrounding boroughs and municipalities (a politically difficult and procedurally cumbersome task). Kentucky's laws were pro-annexation but also provided a poison pill—ready self-incorporation of small subdivi-

TABLE 1.6
BAD STATE LAWS CAN HOBBLE CITIES

Central city	Municipal annexation			Approval by voters		Approval by county government
	Authorized by state law	Begun by property owner petition	Begun by city council	Within annexed area	Within annexing city	
Houston	Yes	Yes	Yes	No	No	No
Detroit	Yes	Yes	[No]	[Yes]	[Yes]	No
Columbus	Yes	Yes	Yes	[Yes]	No	[Yes]
Cleveland	Yes	Yes	Yes	[Yes]	No	[Yes]
Nashville	Yes	Yes	Yes	[Yes]	[Yes]	No
Louisville	Yes	No	Yes	No	No	No
Indianapolis	Yes	Yes	Yes	No	No	No
Milwaukee	Yes	Yes	[No]	[Yes]	No	No
Albuquerque	Yes	Yes	Yes	[Yes]	No	No
Syracuse	Yes[a]	Yes	[No]	[Yes]	No	No
Madison	Yes	Yes	Yes	[Yes]	No	No
Harrisburg	No	n.a.	n.a.	n.a.	n.a.	n.a.
Raleigh	Yes	Yes	Yes	No	No	No
Richmond	Yes[b]	Yes	Yes	No	No	[Yes]
Charlotte	Yes	Yes	Yes	No	No	No
Grand Rapids	Yes	Yes	[No]	[Yes]	[Yes]	No

Note: n.a. = not applicable. Adverse requirements are set off by brackets.
a. The New York annexation law was effectively nullified by a state constitutional amendment requiring voter approval of boundary changes. b. The Virginia annexation law was rendered moot by the legislature's requiring county approval in 1979.

sions facing annexation. After 93 suburban micromunicipalities had been organized, Louisville negotiated a moratorium on both annexations and new incorporations in return for a tax-sharing compact with Jefferson County. Michigan law allowed ready paths for townships to either incorporate as municipalities or become charter townships; in either case, they were protected from annexation by other cities. In 1979, the Virginia General Assembly insulated urban counties from further annexations by "independent cities" such as Richmond (see Box 1.4).

Lesson 9: Neighbors Can Trap Cities

Regardless of annexation laws, in all states (except Nebraska[11]), one municipality cannot annex property within another municipality, regardless of the disparity in size. Typically, this rule is the most insurmountable barrier to annexations by a central city. Thus, many older cities have become gradually surrounded by smaller cities, towns, and villages. Newer central cities often face only farmland, swamp, or sagebrush.

Table 1.7 shows the "elbow room" each of the target cities had. In 1950, no city came close to filling up its home county; central cites covered only from 1 percent to 23 percent of home-county land area. Detroit, nevertheless, was bounded by the Detroit River (an international boundary) and by 15 municipalities enclosing 75 percent of its city limits. Cleveland was completely hemmed in by Lake Erie on the north and by 20 smaller municipalities ringing its city limits. Regardless of state laws, Detroit and Cleveland had nowhere to grow. By contrast, Columbus annexed aggressively, driven by two strategic goals: to become the most populous city in Ohio and never to allow itself to become completely surrounded by incorporated suburbs.

After Milwaukee almost doubled its territory by annexation in the 1950s, all remaining townships in Milwaukee County converted themselves into annexation-proof municipalities. Within the same state, however, Madison was able to slow down the municipalization of its local townships. (Townships are discussed at length in Chapter 3 and Box 3.5.) Like Milwaukee, Grand Rapids almost doubled its territory in the 1950s and 1960s but thereafter was completely trapped within municipalized or charter townships (see Box 1.5).

Houston, Albuquerque, Raleigh, and Charlotte had relatively clear sailing in terms of implementing their annexation strategies.

TABLE 1.7
ELASTIC CITIES HAD ELBOW ROOM TO GROW; INELASTIC CITIES DID NOT

Central city	Home county	City area as a percentage of home county area		Percentage of city limits enclosed by other municipalities, 1950	Number of other municipalities in home county, 1950	Other municipalities as a percentage of home county population, 1950	Number of townships in home county, 1950
		1950	2010				
Houston	Harris	9	35	10	15	11	0
Detroit	Wayne	23	23	75	25	17	17
Columbus	Franklin	7	40	15	24	11	18[a]
Cleveland	Cuyahoga	16	17	100	55	33	5[a]
Nashville	Davidson	4	95	1	3	1	0
Louisville	Jefferson	10	84	30	15	2	0
Indianapolis	Marion	14	91	25	22	4	9
Milwaukee	Milwaukee	21	40	25	10	16	7
Albuquerque	Bernalillo	4	16	0	0	0	0
Syracuse	Onondaga	3	3	100	15	11	[19]
Madison	Dane	1	6	20	24	16	35
Harrisburg	Dauphin	1	2	100	16	20	[23]
Raleigh	Wake	1	17	0	11	9	0
Richmond	Chesterfield/Henrico	5	9	0	1	0.4	n.a.
Charlotte	Mecklenburg	6	56	0	5	3	0
Grand Rapids	Kent	3	5	15	10	6	24

Notes: n.a. = not applicable. Townships with full municipal status are set off by brackets.
a. Only Ohio townships with nonmunicipalized populations are listed.

Lesson 10: Old Cities Are Complacent; Young Cities Are Ambitious

Certainly one clear distinction between elastic and inelastic cities is age; elastic cities are younger than inelastic cities. Table 1.8 lists the census at which each city first exceeded 100,000 inhabitants (or 50,000 in Harrisburg's case, because the city peaked at 89,544 in 1950).

On average, the inelastic cities passed 100,000 or more residents around the mid-1890s, whereas the elastic cities did not reach that milestone until about the early 1930s. An average date of 1932,

TABLE 1.8
INELASTIC CITIES ARE OLDER THAN ARE ELASTIC CITIES

Central city	Census when the population exceeded 100,000
Houston	1920
Detroit	1880
Columbus	1900
Cleveland	1880
Nashville	1910
Louisville	1870
Indianapolis	1890
Milwaukee	1880
Albuquerque	1960
Syracuse	1900
Madison	1970
Harrisburg	1920[a]
Raleigh	1970
Richmond	1910
Charlotte	1940
Grand Rapids	1910

a. Census when the population exceeded 50,000.

Box 1.4 Annexation and the Federal Voting Rights Act

Since 1971, a new hurdle has existed for many municipalities' annexation powers—the federal Voting Rights Act.

Under section 5 of the act, municipalities in all or sections of 29 states with large Black, Hispanic, or Native American populations are required to clear proposed annexations with the U.S. Department of Justice. The federal concern is that by annexing predominantly White outlying areas, municipalities would dilute the growing political strength of Blacks and Hispanics.

In actuality, the Justice Department typically objects to less than 2 percent of all annexations submitted for review. Of these questioned annexations, less than 1 percent are ultimately prevented by either Justice Department objections or the federal courts. Many contested annexations are resolved by changing the political system to enhance minority representation, typically by shifting from at-large to districted local elections.

Perhaps the most famous and bitterly contested annexation was Richmond's annexation of 23 square miles of Chesterfield County in 1970. For seven years thereafter, federal courts blocked further city elections until the case was finally decided by the U.S. Supreme Court.

Opponents charged that by annexing more than 47,000 new residents (97 percent White), the White-dominated Richmond city council had sought to dilute growing Black political power. Proponents argued that the annexation's purpose was to strengthen Richmond's middle-class population; acquire vacant land for residential, commercial, and industrial growth; and expand the tax base to meet Richmond's future revenue needs.

The irony is that both sides were correct. By unanimous vote, the U.S. Supreme Court ruled in 1975 that the annexation "was infected

however, masks an important difference: Houston, Columbus, Nashville, and Indianapolis passed the 100,000 mark only one to four decades after the inelastic cities with which they are paired; Albuquerque, Madison, and Raleigh are truly recent entrants to big-city status.

What transformed the futures of Houston, Columbus, Nashville, and Indianapolis was, in large measure, the attitude of their community leadership (with citizen support). Houston and Columbus were very expansionist through aggressive annexation (despite

by the impermissible purpose of denying the right to vote based on race."[a] The Court allowed the annexation to stand, on the basis of Richmond's shift to a nine-member council elected by wards.

After adding 47,000 new residents (and an estimated one-quarter to its tax base), the 1970 annexation, however, marked the end of Richmond's expansion. Blacks gained a majority of the ward council seats by 1978, electing Henry Marsh as Richmond's first African American mayor.

Richmond's Black community has gained political control of a depreciating asset. While the three adjacent counties have almost tripled with 454,000 new residents, Richmond's population has dropped by more than 45,000, or 18 percent, since 1970. City income growth has steadily lagged suburban income growth. City incomes are now 83 percent of suburban incomes. Much of Richmond's Black middle class has left the city for suburban locations.

Richmond's annexation powers were ended by the Virginia legislature, which in 1979 exempted urban counties from further annexation without county approval. Probably Richmond's Black majority city council would have lost all interest in further annexations in any event so as not to jeopardize its newly acquired political power.

The saga of Richmond's annexation battle epitomizes one of urban America's sad realities. In many cities, achieving political dominance has also trapped many Blacks or Hispanics in cities of declining social and economic opportunity as abandonment of the city by middle-class residents, investors, and employers accelerates.

a. All information on the history of the Richmond annexation dispute is taken from John V. Moeser and Rutledge M. Dennis, *The Politics of Annexation: Oligarchic Power in a Southern City* (Cambridge, MA: Schenkman, 1982). Quotation is from page 172.

limitations on their legal powers). Even more striking, the leadership of Nashville and Indianapolis (and, finally, Louisville) transformed their communities by successful city–county consolidations. Without city–county consolidation, which lifted all three cities out of slow erosion, Nashville and Indianapolis would probably be not much different from unconsolidated Louisville and Milwaukee.

On the eve of the suburban era, older, established cities tended to be complacent. Already centers of national or regional wealth, they focused on dividing the pie rather than on making the pie larger. By

1950, the shift of people, jobs, and power to the suburbs was under way. A failure of initiative from within as well as legal, historical, and political constraints from without contributed to making many older cities inelastic.

By contrast, younger cities were on the make as they entered the postwar era. Certainly, many would benefit from macroeconomic changes (for example, the growth of industry in the Sun Belt). Many would even benefit from technological changes (for example, inexpensive air-conditioning units for Sun Belt homes and offices). But many cities made their own futures by willing their own elasticity.

Box 1.5 How Townships Walled Up Grand Rapids

Every city, of course, begins small. In 1831, original settler Louis Campeau bought 72 acres of what is now the entire downtown business district from the federal government for $90 and named his tract Grand Rapids.

Over the decades, the city of Grand Rapids (incorporated in 1850) annexed land within its four contiguous townships. (Because Michigan is a "little boxes" state, 872-square-mile Kent County was originally divided into 24 townships.) By 1950, Grand Rapids had grown steadily through annexation to 23.4 square miles with a population of 176,515.

As an already incorporated municipality (in 1891), the city of East Grand Rapids was immunized from any annexations by Grand Rapids. However, the contiguous townships (Grand Rapids, Paris, Wyoming, and Walker) were the central city's expansion targets. Yet each township had substantial, already urbanized populations; in 1950, the central city accounted for barely half the urbanized land and 78 percent of the urbanized population.

Moreover, long-established township governments were not inclined to acquiesce in being annexed out of existence by an expanding Grand Rapids. A series of bitter annexation wars ensued[a] in which Grand Rapids succeeded in almost doubling its municipal territory to 44.9 square miles by 1970 and raising its population to 197,649.

But the embattled townships took steps to inoculate themselves legally against further annexations. First, three townships followed the example of East Grand Rapids by themselves becoming incorporated cities: Wyoming Township became the city of Wyoming in 1959, Walker Township became the city of Walker in 1962, and the city of Kentwood was incorporated in 1967 from what remained of Paris Township (according to its website) "to prevent further

---

Lesson 11: Racial Prejudice
Has Shaped Growth Patterns

Both racial prejudice and discriminatory public policies played a major role in the evolution of overwhelmingly White suburbs surrounding increasingly Black and Hispanic inelastic cities (see Box 1.6 on redlining minority neighborhoods).

Certainly some new suburbanites were motivated by nonracial considerations. Many middle-class families moved because older cities lacked dream houses at affordable prices in good neighbor-

---

annexation of land from the adjacent cities of Grand Rapids and Wyoming."

Second, in 1947, the Michigan legislature created "charter townships," a special township classification supposedly "to provide additional powers and streamlined administration" for governing growing, urbanizing communities. However, "A primary motivation for townships to adopt the charter form," the Michigan Township Association states candidly on its website, "is to provide greater protection against annexation by a city."

As an anti-annexation "poison pill," Plainfield Township converted to a charter township in 1978 as Grand Rapids' successful annexation of portions of Grand Rapids Township had reached Plainfield's township boundary. What remained of Grand Rapids Township became a charter township in 1979.

By 1980, the city of Grand Rapids was completely surrounded by either incorporated municipalities (Wyoming, Walker, Kentwood, and East Grand Rapids) or charter townships (Grand Rapids and Plainfield). Had Grand Rapids been able to continue to annex these communities totally under Michigan law, it would today be a city of 167.8 square miles and about 389,000 residents, with continuing prospects for annexation of other township lands.[b]

a. For instance, a Wyoming Township official once blocked Grand Rapids from annexing the former Kelvinator factory located in Wyoming Township by moving his son into a mobile home on the property, which otherwise had no residents. Under Michigan law, that forced a vote in which the supervisor's son cast the only (and deciding) vote against annexation.

b. Grand Rapids' access to Ada Township is blocked by only a 600-yard-wide strip of Plainfield Charter Township, but from a legal perspective that narrow strip might as well be the Iron Curtain.

Box 1.6 Suburbs Segregated by the Federal Government

"For Whites Only" was the sign that the federal government hung out as America's suburbs exploded with millions of new families in the postwar decades. The federal government did not create discrimination in America's housing markets, but it institutionalized it on an unprecedented scale.[a]

In 1933, as millions of owners were losing their homes during the Great Depression, the New Deal created the Home Owners' Loan Corporation (HOLC). To help struggling families meet mortgage payments, HOLC offered low-interest, long-term mortgage loans. HOLC developed a rating system to evaluate the risks associated with loans made to specific urban neighborhoods. HOLC designated four categories of neighborhood risk; on its "residential security maps" the highest-risk areas were colored red. Black neighborhoods were always coded red; even those with small Black percentages were usually rated as "hazardous" and denied loans.

HOLC's loan program was small, but the impact of its discriminatory practices was enormous. During the 1930s and 1940s, HOLC residential security maps were widely followed by private banks for their own loan practices. When the Federal Housing Administration (FHA) and the Veterans Administration (VA) were founded (in 1937 and 1944, respectively), they embraced HOLC's underwriting practices. The 1939 FHA *Underwriting Manual*, for example, stated that "if a neighborhood is to retain stability, it is necessary that the properties shall continue to be occupied by the same social and racial classes."[b]

FHA and VA largely financed the rapid suburbanization of the United States after World War II. The federal government's regulations favored construction of single-family homes but discouraged the building of multifamily apartments. As a result, the vast majority of FHA and VA mortgages went to new, White, middle-

---

hoods with good schools. Others moved to flee high city taxes and low city politics or to live nearer to their suburban jobs.

Yet in many metro areas, racially motivated "White flight" was undeniably a major factor. "Good" neighborhoods with "good" schools often were seen as neighborhoods and schools without Blacks and, to a lesser degree, without Hispanics. After the civil rights revolution in the 1960s, neighborhoods and schools without *poor* Blacks and *poor* Hispanics increasingly satisfied the "good" test.

Having escaped "city problems," most suburbanites vigorously resisted city annexation, often by incorporating their new com-

class suburban neighborhoods, and very few were awarded to Black neighborhoods in central cities. Historian Kenneth Jackson found that from 1934 to 1960, suburban St. Louis County received six times as much FHA mortgage money per capita as did the city of St. Louis. Per capita FHA lending in suburban Long Island was 11 times greater than in Brooklyn and 60 times greater than in the Bronx.

Such government practices died hard. As late as 1950, FHA was still encouraging the use of restrictive racial covenants—two years after the U.S. Supreme Court had ruled them unconstitutional! FHA's redlining continued overtly until the mid-1960s, when Robert Weaver became the first African American secretary of the U.S. Department of Housing and Urban Development. The weak Civil Rights Act of 1968 finally outlawed housing discrimination. However, the full extent of discrimination in mortgage lending was revealed only after passage of the Home Mortgage Disclosure Act (1975), and significant mortgage funds began to flow back into inner-city neighborhoods only with vigorous enforcement of the Community Reinvestment Act (1977).

Extreme segregation of America's housing markets was not the result of some "natural" process of self-segregation. For decades it was force fed by discriminatory "rules of the game" from federal, state, and local governments.

a. This discussion is adapted from Chapter 2 of Douglas S. Massey and Nancy A. Denton, *American Apartheid: Segregation and the Making of the Underclass* (Cambridge, MA: Harvard University Press, 1993), which, in turn, cites extensively from Kenneth T. Jackson, *Crabgrass Frontier: the Suburbanization of the United States* (New York: Oxford University Press, 1985).

b. Federal Housing Authority, *Underwriting Manual* (Washington, DC: Government Printing Office, 1939).

munities. More recently, many city Blacks and Hispanics—finally taking control of city hall—also resisted city expansion, especially where past annexations had been instruments of maintaining White control (revisit Box 1.4).

* * *

History, geography, state laws, civic leadership (or lack of same), and racial attitudes all shaped the elasticity or inelasticity of cities.

What were the demographic, social, economic, and fiscal consequences of being an inelastic rather than an elastic city?

Lesson 12: Elastic Cities "Capture" Suburban Population Growth; Inelastic Cities "Contribute" to Suburban Population Growth

Postwar growth has been primarily suburban style, low-density
development emphasizing detached, single-family homes. At the
outset of the postwar period, elastic cities had large inventories of
undeveloped land or would be able to annex either undeveloped
land or new subdivisions. They captured much of this suburban-
style growth within their own municipal boundaries.

Inelastic cities could not grow through either infill or annexation.
They could not compete with new suburbs in offering the desired
suburban-style model for family life. Incapable of capturing a share
of suburban-type development, inelastic cities actually contributed
White middle-class families to the new suburbs. In recent years, a
rapidly growing Black middle class has moved to the suburbs as
well in many regions.

Table 1.9 sums up the effect in terms of a city's "capture/contrib-
ute" percentage. The capture/contribute percentage is calculated by
dividing a city's net population change by the metro area's net population change. In effect, Table 1.9 measures a city's success or failure
in competing for middle-class families with its suburbs.

Over the past 60 years, Houston captured 31 percent of its region's
net new residents, whereas Detroit contributed −101 percent of its
suburbs' net new residents; in effect, over the six decades, Detroit's
population loss (−1,135,791 residents) was slightly greater than the
metro area's population gain (+1,125,935 residents). Columbus captured 38 percent whereas Cleveland contributed −57 percent of its
suburbs' population growth, and so forth.

During the past decade, the city of Detroit's role as a net contribu-
tor was reemphasized in circumstances in which the entire Detroit
region lost population. For the decade, Detroit's population loss (an
astounding loss of 237,493 residents, or one-quarter of its population, in just one decade) was 52 percent greater than its region's
population loss of 156,307 residents; hence, the city's capture/con-
tribute percentage was −152 percent. Similarly, during the decade,
Cleveland lost more residents (81,588) than its region (70,903) for a
capture/contribute percentage of −115 percent.

Table 1.9
Elastic Cities *Capture* Suburban Population Growth; Inelastic
Cities *Contribute* to Suburban Population Growth

	City capture/contribute percentage	
Central city	1950–2010	2000s
Houston	+31	+12
Detroit	−101	−152
Columbus	+38	+34
Cleveland	−57	−115
Nashville	+41	+12
Louisville (to 2000)	−25	−13
Louisville–Jefferson County (to 2010)	+39	+281
Indianapolis	+39	+12
Milwaukee	−8	−4
Albuquerque	+64	+62
Syracuse	−38	−17
Madison	+40	+38
Harrisburg	−17	+1
Raleigh	+27	+21
Richmond	−4	+4
Charlotte	+48	+45
Grand Rapids	+3	−29

At the other end of the spectrum, through city–county consolidation, the former city of Louisville seemingly gained 342,406 residents since 2000 by absorbing all the population in unincorporated Jefferson County. The city's gain compared with a net regional population gain of 121,591 for a city capture/contribute percentage of +281 percent. Though just a statistical abstraction, the consolidated city's enhanced tax base and newly acquired in-

TABLE 1.10
Elastic Cities Gain Population; Inelastic Cities Lose Population

Central city	City population		Percentage change	
	1950	2010	1950–2010	2000s
Houston	596,163	2,099,451	+252	+7
Detroit	1,849,568	713,777	−61	−25
Columbus	375,901	787,033	+109	+11
Cleveland	914,808	396,815	−57	−17
Nashville	174,307	601,222	+245	+10
Louisville (to 2000)	369,129	256,231	−31	−5
Louisville–Jefferson County	n.a.	597,337	+62	+133
Indianapolis	427,173	820,445	+92	+4
Milwaukee	637,392	594,833	−7	0
Albuquerque	96,815	545,852	+464	+22
Syracuse	220,583	145,170	−34	−1
Madison	96,056	233,209	+143	+12
Harrisburg	89,544	49,528	−45	+1
Raleigh	65,679	403,892	+515	+46
Richmond	230,310	204,214	−11	+3
Charlotte	134,042	731,424	+446	+35
Grand Rapids	176,515	188,040	+7	−5

Note: n.a. = not applicable.

ventory of undeveloped land will pay big dividends in coming decades.

Lesson 13: Elastic Cities Gain Population; Inelastic Cities Lose Population

As Table 1.3 documented, all our sample metro areas grew in population from 1950 to 2010. As Table 1.10 makes agonizingly clear, however, in the Age of Sprawl, inelastic cities suffered catastrophic population losses. With the exception of Grand Rapids, inelastic cities lost from 7 percent (Milwaukee) to 61 percent (Detroit) of their inhabitants. Metro population growth occurred entirely in suburbs outside these cities' boundaries. Though some inelastic cities recovered population from Hispanic or Asian immigration or gentrification in recent decades, the effect for Milwaukee, Syracuse, Harrisburg, and Richmond was minor.

In sharp contrast, elastic cities grew dramatically. Columbus, Indianapolis, and Madison doubled, and Houston and Nashville tripled their city populations. Albuquerque's and Charlotte's populations increased fivefold and Raleigh's sixfold. All continued to grow during the 2000s (six at double-digit rates of increase).

Lesson 14: Shrinking Household Size Understates Elastic Cities' Gains While Overstating Inelastic Cities' Losses

Over the past 60 years, the average U.S. household size has shrunk 25 percent (see Box 1.7). In effect, a city would have had to add one-quarter more households just to maintain its 1950 population level. As a result, as Table 1.11 shows, elastic cities and their regions have grown even more than mere population changes document. Whereas metro Raleigh's population increased 384 percent, for example, its households increased by 668 percent; the city itself, which annexed land rapidly, grew 6-fold in population (515 percent) but 10-fold in households (908 percent).

Similarly, even inelastic regions of the so-called Rust Belt experienced a near doubling or more of their households from the lowest increase (metro Cleveland: 75 percent) to the highest increase (Grand Rapids: 164 percent).

Household trends are important because they define overall housing demand. In fact, adding in the need to building new housing units to replace deteriorated or obsolescent housing, homebuilders could look to rising demand even in slowly growing markets (in population terms).

From city hall's perceptive, households are also residential property taxpayers. Although a Milwaukee or Richmond or preconsolidation Louisville may have experienced population loss, it actually gained households. Only Detroit, Cleveland, Harrisburg, and Syracuse suffered crippling loss of residential taxpayers.

Box 1.7 Population Change: What Does It *Really* Tell Us?

When we envision our nation's capital, we often imagine a city of pencil skirts, suit coats, and briefcases. We see the clash between Red and Blue and the hustle and bustle of an apparently prosperous city. These are the images that often first come to mind for many Americans, including D.C. interns like myself, when thinking about Washington, D.C.

What would they say, however, when they learn that over the past 60 years D.C. has lost more than 200,000 people? Even more perplexing, how would they respond to the 19 percent gain in households since 1950 despite a 25 percent drop in population?

By comparing both population counts and counts of occupied housing units between 1950 and 2010,[a] one sees clearly that city population decline in inelastic cities is greater than the decrease in number of households, and population growth is less than household growth in elastic cities.

For example, inelastic cities such as St. Louis, Baltimore, and Washington, D.C., have decreased in population from 1950 to 2010 by 63 percent, 35 percent, and 25 percent, respectively. However, during the same period, their percentage change in households showed much less of a decline, with St. Louis and Baltimore losing 45 percent and 7 percent, respectively, and Washington, D.C., surprisingly gaining 19 percent in household counts.

Conversely, elastic cities showed household growth greater than the change in population. For example, from 1950 to 2010, Charlotte impressively increased its population by 446 percent (a more than fivefold increase) but expanded by 686 percent (almost eightfold) in household units.

Thus, for the central cities in the 137 MSAs analyzed, inelastic cities proportionally declined more in population than in households, and elastic cities increased more in households than in population.

Additionally, the average household size in metro areas has decreased since 1950 by roughly one-quarter. For some cities, for example, an increase in immigration can mean more individuals searching for single apartments, such as New York City, which has historically served as a port of entry to immigrants. For others, a smaller average household size results from the current overall trend, in contrast with 60 years ago, for families to have fewer children and not have extended family members live with them.

Still another phenomenon is the increase of young professionals entering some cities. Despite being in the zero-elasticity category and losing a significant portion of its black population, D.C. has seen a net increase of 30,000 people in the past decade. Primarily because of the draw to downtown D.C. for employment and an increasingly urbane lifestyle, more than 50,000 Whites have migrated into the city. In fact, since 1970, Whites migrating into D.C. have increased steadily. This White gentrification added to the population, but it increased the number of households even more, because most of the migrants were single, young professionals. From 1990 to 2009, the number of householders living alone increased from 103,600 to 117,435. In Census 2010, 44 percent of all households living in D.C. consisted of single-person householders.

A correlation also exists between city density and average household size. In 1950, more dense cities, such as New York, D.C., and Baltimore, had smaller household sizes of 3.4 persons per household in comparison with less dense cities, which, on average, had 3.6 persons per household. A very dense city, New York, had 10,275 households per square mile as of 2010. Other older cities, such as San Francisco and Washington, D.C., exhibited a higher ratio of households per square mile as well, with 7,378 and 4,369, respectively.

In comparison, the elastic, less dense city of Charlotte had only 974 households per square mile. Overall, less dense cities such as Charlotte offer more space for family-friendly housing, whereas more dense cities, such as D.C., must build upward and attract young professionals and empty nesters in search of apartments. Thus, the ability of less dense, more elastic cities to expand outwardly creates slightly larger household sizes, while more dense cities must develop vertically.

This phenomenon is of great importance to municipal governments. More households means more residential taxpayers. Although family households may have more mouths to feed and children to clothe, single-person households typically have more discretionary income to spend.

When you now envision the nation's capital, you may now imagine an increasing number of single-person households, swarms of professionals racing to the Metro, and interns like me packing into federal buildings.

—Ashley Engel

a. The 1950 census did not tabulate "households" but reported "occupied housing units." Census reports in subsequent decades clearly show that "occupied housing units" and "households" are synonymous.

TABLE 1.11
SHRINKING HOUSEHOLD SIZE UNDERSTATES ELASTIC CITIES' GAINS
WHILE OVERSTATING INELASTIC CITIES' LOSSES

Metro area	Metro area		Central city	
	Percentage change in population, 1950–2010	Percentage change in households, 1950–2010	Percentage change in population, 1950–2010	Percentage change in households, 1950–2010
Houston	+445	+547	+252	+333
Detroit	+36	+93	−61	−47
Columbus	+146	+235	+109	+202
Cleveland	+24	+75	−57	−37
Nashville	+185	+305	+245	+401
Louisville (to 2000)	n.a.	n.a.	−31	+2
Louisville–Jefferson County (to 2010)	+83	+229	+62	+127
Indianapolis	+132	+196	+92	+152
Milwaukee	+53	+116	−7	+24
Albuquerque	+395	+596	+464	+780
Syracuse	+42	+99	−34	−10
Madison	+155	+283	+143	+294
Harrisburg	+73	+145	−45	−25
Raleigh	+384	+668	+515	+908
Richmond	+137	+252	−11	+35
Charlotte	+243	+414	+446	+686
Grand Rapids	+115	+164	+7	+33

Note: n.a. = not applicable.

Lesson 15: Inelastic Areas Are
More Segregated Than Elastic Areas

The high concentration of Blacks and Hispanics—particularly *poor* Blacks and *poor* Hispanics—in inelastic central cities dominated their regions' social geography and shaped decisively the choices that middle-class families (White and Black) made about where to live and work. Table 1.12 illustrates the significant differences be-

TABLE 1.12
INELASTIC AREAS ARE MORE RACIALLY SEGREGATED
THAN ARE ELASTIC AREAS

Metro area	Percentage Black, 2010			Metro segregation index, 2010[a]	30-year index change
	Metro area	City	Suburbs		
Houston	17	23	13	61	−13
Detroit	23	82	11	74	−14
Columbus	15	28	5	60	−13
Cleveland	20	52	12	73	−13
Nashville	15	28	7	55	−10
Louisville (to 2000)	14	33	8	56	−17
Louisville–Jefferson County (to 2010)	14	23	6	n.a.	n.a.
Indianapolis	15	27	4	65	−14
Milwaukee	16	39	2	80	−4
Albuquerque	2	3	1	29	−11
Syracuse	8	28	2	65	−10
Madison	4	7	3	46	+1
Harrisburg	10	50	6	63	−11
Raleigh	20	29	15	41	−5
Richmond	29	50	25	52	−11
Charlotte	24	34	16	53	−5
Grand Rapids	8	20	4	61	−15

Note: n.a. = not applicable.
a. Segregation index: scale 0 to 100 (100 = total apartheid).

tween inelastic areas and elastic areas in terms of residential segregation of Blacks.

Each metropolitan pairing (except Charlotte–Grand Rapids) had roughly similar percentages of Blacks. Sharply different metro growth patterns yielded sharply different racial populations for central cities.

In 2010, metro Houston, for example, was 17 percent Black. Many of its new "suburbs" lay within Houston's expanding city limits. As a result, the city of Houston was only 23 percent Black. Metro Detroit had a somewhat higher Black population (23 percent) than did metro Houston. With virtually all postwar subdivisions (to which Detroit's White residents moved) built outside its city limits, the city of Detroit was 82 percent Black. Houston's Black

---

Box 1.8 Calculating Relative Segregation

An indispensable resource for tracking racial, ethnic, and economic disparities is the US2010 website of Brown University (http://www.s4.brown.edu/us2010/Data/Data.htm#WP).[a] Using metro area definitions for Census 2010, US2010's website provides easy-to-view sortable lists and downloadable tables calculating various segregation indices for 368 metro areas (and 29 metro divisions within the largest metro areas) for 1980, 1990, 2000, and 2010.

Overall topical areas and their brief descriptions are as follows:

- *Residential segregation by race or ethnicity.* Population data (all ages) for non-Hispanic White, non-Hispanic Black, Hispanic, and Asian are provided that include differences in residential patterns of one racial or ethnic group in relation to another (dissimilarity index) and the racial or ethnic composition of the tract where the average member of a particular group lives (exposure index). Also shown is the percentage of same-group population in the census tract where the average member of a racial or ethnic group lives (isolation index).
- *Separate and unequal.* These data describe the characteristics of neighborhoods where the average member of each racial or ethnic group lives. There are links to pages that explore how neighborhood differences are related to people's characteristics other than race or ethnicity: their income and nativity (comparing U.S.-born to foreign-born group members).
- *School segregation by race or ethnicity.* Enrollment data for non-Hispanic White, Black, Hispanic, and Asian elementary

population proportionally was less than twice its suburbs' Black population (13 percent); however, Detroit's Black population was proportionally more than seven times its suburbs' Black population (11 percent).

One might expect the demographic profile of an elastic city to reflect fairly closely the demographic profile of its metro area, because, by definition, an elastic city encompasses much of its region. However, the metropolitan Black segregation index used in the last two columns of Table 1.12 is calculated on a census tract–by–census tract basis *as if political boundaries did not exist* (see Box 1.8). On a scale of 0 to 100 (with 100 = total apartheid), metro Detroit, among its neighborhoods region-wide, was much more residentially segregated (an index score of 74) than was metro Houston (61) in 2010.

---

schoolchildren in metro areas and school districts across the nation are provided that include differences in enrollment patterns of one racial or ethnic group in relation to another (dissimilarity index), the racial or ethnic composition of the elementary school that the average child of a particular group attends (exposure and isolation indices), and the percentile ranking on state standardized tests (in 2004) of the school that the average child of a racial or ethnic group attends.

- *Income segregation.* These data describe the extent of family income segregation in metropolitan areas. They include several different measures of family income for all metropolitan areas from 1970 through the 2005–09 American Community Survey, based on the current metropolitan boundaries

To emphasize how these conditions are spatially organized, the project has developed web-based GIS (Geographic Information System) mapping systems that allow users to build and analyze maps via the Internet. Map USA (http://maps.s4.brown.edu/mapusa/) provides data on census tracts throughout the entire United States. Map US Schools (http://www.s4.brown.edu/usschools/) provides information about public schools and school districts across the nation, including racial and class composition of students and student achievement. All these systems call attention to the concentrations of advantage and disadvantage that are typical of American communities.

a. US2010 was begun by Professor John Logan as the American Communities Project when he was at the Lewis Mumford Center at the State University of New York–Albany.

Racial segregation in inelastic areas was consistently higher. Black segregation was always less within an elastic metro area than it was within its paired inelastic metro area. Between metro areas in different sections of the country (for example, Houston–Detroit, Albuquerque–Syracuse), differences in racial patterns might be explained in terms of broad sectional differences (Sun Belt–Frost Belt, for example). The differences, however, held true between metro areas in the same section (Raleigh–Richmond, Nashville–Louisville) and even within the same state (Columbus–Cleveland).

The good news, as indicated in the last column, is that the level of Black segregation has been steadily coming down; 40 years ago, for example, most of these regions had Black segregation index scores in the 80s and low 90s.[12] The bad news is that for African Americans and other Blacks, the level of residential segregation in most regions is still very high—well beyond that initially experienced historically by any immigrant group.

Lesson 16: Major Immigration Increases Hispanic Segregation

In 2010, Hispanics were significantly less segregated than were Blacks (Table 1.13). Typically, the level of Hispanic residential segregation was 10 to 20 points below Black segregation within the same metro area.

However, whereas Black segregation declined everywhere in the past three decades (except Madison), Hispanic segregation increased almost everywhere. Only in Albuquerque, whose Hispanic ancestors settled New Mexico a generation before the Pilgrims landed on Plymouth Rock, did Hispanic residential segregation decline significantly (−9 index points) since 1980.

The factor driving higher Hispanic segregation was major immigration. With the exception of Houston (14 percent) and Albuquerque (36 percent), as late as 1980 the Hispanic population was still negligible in the other 14 regions. Thereafter, immigration exploded. Hispanic immigrants moved toward job opportunities. Major growth centers saw staggering increases in the numbers of Hispanic residents, such as Indianapolis (a 12-fold increase), Nashville (a 15-fold increase), Charlotte (a 26-fold increase), and Raleigh (a 38-fold increase). All four regions experienced double-digit increases in their Hispanic segregation index.

TABLE 1.13
MAJOR IMMIGRATION INCREASES HISPANIC SEGREGATION

Metro area	Metro percentage Hispanic		Metro Hispanic growth, 1980–2010	Metro Hispanic segregation index, 2010[a]	30-year index change
	1980	2010			
Houston	14	35	364	53	+5
Detroit	2	4	135	43	+2
Columbus	1	4	718	41	+15
Cleveland	2	5	151	52	−6
Nashville	1	7	1,638	48	+26
Louisville	1	4	820	39	+16
Indianapolis	1	6	1,125	47	+20
Milwaukee	2	9	330	57	+2
Albuquerque	36	47	152	36	−9
Syracuse	1	3	301	42	+7
Madison	1	5	836	40	+15
Harrisburg	1	5	463	47	−1
Raleigh	1	10	3,723	37	+17
Richmond	1	5	774	45	+10
Charlotte	1	10	2,516	48	+19
Grand Rapids	2	8	548	50	+8

a. Segregation index: scale 0 to 100 (100 = total apartheid).

Though slowed by the Great Recession toward the end of the 2000s, the growth of the Hispanic population continued in almost all areas of the country where economic opportunity could be found.

One hopes that higher Hispanic segregation levels will be a temporary phenomenon, reflecting the tendency of new immigrants to band together in port-of-entry neighborhoods. Where the Hispanic population is relatively stable, residential segregation declines as succeeding generations fan out into a wider range of neighborhoods (as Albuquerque illustrates despite a doubling of its Hispanic population).

Lesson 17: Highly Racially Segregated Regions Are Also Highly Economically Segregated Regions

Table 1.14 presents a variation on the segregation index as in Tables 1.12 and 1.13, but it is based on patterns of income distribution.[13] We find that economic segregation largely tracked racial segregation. Inelastic areas were somewhat more economically segregated than elastic areas. In fact, Detroit, Cleveland, and Milwaukee were the sixth, eighth, and ninth most economically segregated metropolitan areas in the country in 2009.

TABLE 1.14

HIGHLY RACIALLY SEGREGATED REGIONS ARE ALSO HIGHLY ECONOMICALLY SEGREGATED REGIONS

Metro area	Metro economic segregation index[a]				
	1969	1979	1989	1999	2009
Houston	35	35	40	38	41
Detroit	31	34	45	38	45
Columbus	35	33	42	39	42
Cleveland	33	35	48	42	45
Nashville	36	30	38	36	40
Louisville	35	33	41	37	40
Indianapolis	29	30	37	34	38
Milwaukee	30	34	49	43	43
Albuquerque	27	26	33	31	32
Syracuse	25	26	33	32	36
Madison	25	23	28	27	28
Harrisburg	22	22	27	27	29
Raleigh	33	30	35	32	31
Richmond	37	31	41	38	40
Charlotte	33	29	34	35	38
Grand Rapids	27	24	33	29	31

a. Segregation index: scale 0 to 100 (100 = total apartheid).

Thus, although barriers based on race have been coming down in regional housing markets, barriers based on income have been going up. Jim Crow by income is replacing Jim Crow by race.

Lesson 18: Inelastic Cities Have Wide Income Gaps with Their Suburbs; Elastic Cities Maintain Greater City–Suburb Balance

Sixty years ago, all central cities had about the same median[14] family incomes as their metro areas (Table 1.15). Over the next six decades, the median family income of all cities except the very elastic Albuquerque, Madison, Raleigh, Charlotte, and Nashville dropped well below the metropolitan median family income levels. However, with so many middle-class families having left, family incomes in inelastic cities fell far below the metro medians—in effect, even farther below suburban median family incomes.

The city-to-suburb per capita income percentage is the single most important indicator of an urban area's social health. (Unlike median family income, per capita income reflects incomes of wealthier individuals and single-person households.) By 2010, income levels in inelastic cities fell well below those in suburban levels, ranging from lows for Detroit, Milwaukee, and Cleveland (52, 56, and 58 percent, respectively) to highs for Grand Rapids and Richmond (79 and 87 percent). Elastic cities, however, kept pace better with suburban levels, averaging 96 percent of suburban levels. In fact, in 2010, city residents in Raleigh (101 percent), Nashville and Albuquerque (105 percent), and most spectacularly, Charlotte (119 percent) were wealthier than suburban residents.

During the past two decades, the city-to-suburb per capita income percentage declined for most cities. However, the modest movement of young professionals and empty nesters back to the city, plus growing lower-income populations in many older, inner suburbs, pushed some city-suburban income percentages higher—at the lower end, Cleveland and Richmond; at the higher end, Houston, Nashville, and Charlotte.

Lesson 19: Poverty Is More Disproportionately Concentrated in Inelastic Cities Than in Elastic Cities

What about poverty levels? Historically, the South and the West have been lower income regions than the Northeast and Midwest, and to-

TABLE 1.15
INELASTIC CITIES HAVE WIDE INCOME GAP WITH SUBURBS; ELASTIC
CITIES MAINTAIN GREATER CITY–SUBURB BALANCE

Metro area	City percentage of metro median family income		City percentage of suburban per capita income	
	1950	2010	1990	2010
Houston	97	75	89	92
Detroit	99	52	53	52
Columbus	98	80	81	77
Cleveland	91	55	53	58
Nashville	85	90	98	105
Louisville (to 2000)	99	74	79	77
Louisville–Jefferson County (to 2010)	n.a.	92	n.a.	91
Indianapolis	98	81	90	79
Milwaukee	97	61	62	56
Albuquerque	106	100	118	105
Syracuse	100	60	77	63
Madison	109	96	95	89
Harrisburg	101	52	72	63
Raleigh	119	95	103	101
Richmond	97	69	83	87
Charlotte	102	99	96	119
Grand Rapids	98	78	68	79

Note: n.a. = not applicable.

day that pattern persists (Table 1.16). A slightly higher percentage of the population fell below the poverty line in southern and western areas (10.1 percent in 2009) than in northeastern and midwestern areas (9.8 percent). However, poverty was much more concentrated in the inelastic cities (25 percent) than in the elastic cities (13 percent).

TABLE 1.16
POVERTY IS MORE DISPROPORTIONATELY CONCENTRATED IN INELASTIC
CITIES THAN IN ELASTIC CITIES

Metro area	Poverty rate, 2005–09		City fair share of poverty index	
	Metro area	City	2005–09	1969
Houston	11.9	17.3	146	109
Detroit	10.5	28.3	269	174
Columbus	9.3	14.8	159	129
Cleveland	10.3	25.4	247	194
Nashville	9.0	12.3	137	93
Louisville (to 2000)	11.6	21.6	198	151
Louisville–Jefferson County (to 2010)	10.1	13.2	131	n.a.
Indianapolis	8.8	13.5	154	109
Milwaukee	9.1	19.9	219	142
Albuquerque	11.2	11.2	100	85
Syracuse	9.4	25.1	269	138
Madison	5.2	8.1	156	98
Harrisburg	6.1	26.8	439	226
Raleigh	7.0	8.8	126	92
Richmond	7.2	17.8	247	149
Charlotte	8.8	9.4	107	113
Grand Rapids	7.7	17.2	223	146
Average for elastic cities			135	104
Average for inelastic cities			273	165

Note: n.a. = not applicable.

In part, the pattern is sectional. In the South and the West, many poor households still live in rural and semi-urban sections of the metro areas. Poverty is both more spread out in the countryside and more dispersed within the urbanized area itself.

But concentrated poverty is also the result of cities' inelasticity, which magnifies economic segregation. A simple measure of disproportionate concentration of poverty in a central city is what I have called a city's "fair share of poverty index." The index is the ratio between the city's percentage of poor residents and the total metro area's percentage of poor residents. (A city's "fair share" would be reflected as an index of 100.)

In 2009, elastic cities were home to only slightly more than their fair share of the metro area poor (average index: 135). By contrast, inelastic cities had almost three times their fair share of their region's poor (average index: 273). At the extremes, elastic Albuquerque had an index of 100 (exactly equal to its fair share of poverty), whereas inelastic Harrisburg had more than four times its fair share of poverty (index: 439).

Nor is this a temporary phenomenon of the Great Recession. Since the 1970 census (when poverty data were first collected), fair share of poverty indices have risen for all cities decade by decade. However, for elastic cities the increase has been gradual, and elastic cities still maintain reasonable balance (from an average index of 104 in 1969 to 135 in 2009). For inelastic cities, the average index has risen almost three times as fast (from 165 in 1969 to 273 in 2009) and created a serious disparity between central city and suburban poverty.

Lesson 20: Little Boxes Regions Foster Segregation; Big Box Regions Facilitate Integration

"Public policy dictates where development occurs," states the National Association of Home Builders.[15] Local government plans, zoning maps, and investments in public facilities have a major impact on who lives, works, shops, and plays where.

As Table 1.17 shows, local governance in inelastic regions was highly fragmented. The inelastic central cities contained one-quarter or less of the regional population (with the exception of Milwaukee). They were surrounded by myriad incorporated, "little boxes" suburban governments. (With Virginia's unique system of strong county governments and independent cities, metro Richmond was the exception.) Because

Table 1.17
Little Boxes Regions Foster Segregation;
Big Box Regions Facilitate Integration

Metro area	Percentage of metro population governed by central city	Number of suburban governments, 2002	Black segregation index, 2010	Economic segregation index, 2010
Houston	35	149	61	41
Detroit	17	212	74	45
Columbus	43	152	60	42
Cleveland	19	141	73	45
Nashville	38	64	55	40
Louisville (to 2000)	25	156	n.a.	n.a.
Louisville–Jefferson County	47	156[a]	56	40
Indianapolis	47	73[a]	65	38
Milwaukee	38	91	80	43
Albuquerque	62	20	29	32
Syracuse	22	96	65	36
Madison	41	124	46	28
Harrisburg	9	102	63	29
Raleigh	36	31	41	31
Richmond	16	32	52	40
Charlotte	42	62	53	38
Grand Rapids	24	115	61	31

Note: n.a. = not applicable.
a. Indiana townships are excluded as not being units of local general government.

all net growth was occurring outside the central cities, little boxes suburban governments shaped land development policy.

Elastic regions had more unified governance. The central city was a "Big Box," where city hall typically served around 40 percent of the region's inhabitants. Elastic cities had relatively fewer suburban governments as rivals. Many suburban municipalities were small crossroads towns located some distance from the city. Central cities often substantially controlled regional development through annexation and utility policies.

Why should patterns of local governance have any impact on racial and economic segregation? One factor is a local government's sense of constituency. In my experience, the unspoken mission of most little boxes town councils (and most little boxes school boards) is "to keep our town (and our schools) just the way they are for people just like *us*" — whoever *us* happens to be. In earlier decades, local policies to keep out "the Other" could be very overt. In the post–civil rights revolution era, many suburban governments now use planning and zoning powers more subtly. They may require large minimum lot sizes for new homes or ban apartment construction outright, for example, to exclude lower-income households, including many minorities.

Mayors and city councils of elastic Big Box cities are not all Boy Scouts and Girl Scouts, but they do represent broader, more diverse constituencies. As a result, Big Box governments do not adopt exclusionary policies as readily as do little boxes governments; Big Box mayors and councils are accountable to the very voters that would otherwise be excluded. Governance counts.

The way a metro area was governed was not the only factor affecting integration. Another factor was age. Old cities generally had more decaying neighborhoods in which poor Blacks and Hispanics were concentrated. Younger cities emerged in an era of somewhat more enlightened racial attitudes and some effective civil rights laws.

Does greater socioeconomic integration automatically flow from greater governmental unity? Probably not. What is clear is that, absent federal or state mandates, a metro area in which local government is highly fragmented is usually incapable of adopting broad, integrating strategies. Conversely, a metro area in which key planning and zoning powers are concentrated under a dominant local government has the potential to implement policies to promote greater racial and economic integration if that government has the vision and courage to do so.

Lesson 21: Little Boxes School Districts Foster Segregation; Big Box School Districts Facilitate Integration

Table 1.18 shows that how public education was organized largely paralleled how local governance was organized.[16] The school district serving a central city was typically a region's largest school district. In inelastic regions, the city school district, trapped within fixed boundaries, slowly shrank in enrollment and was surrounded by multiple suburban systems.

In elastic regions, the city school district might expand as the city annexed new property—but not always. Some city governments found that guaranteeing residents of to-be-annexed areas that their neighborhoods would remain part of their "suburban" school districts smoothed the path to annexation; Houston, Columbus, and Indianapolis all had "city school districts" much smaller than their expanding city limits. By contrast, Nashville, Albuquerque, and Raleigh were served by unified, county-wide districts.

Table 1.18 also measures school segregation metro-wide by the same dissimilarity index used to measure residential segregation metro-wide. With one exception, Black students were much less segregated in elastic area schools than they were in inelastic area schools. The exception was Louisville, where, in 1975, a federal court ordered the merger of the Louisville and Jefferson County school districts.

Skeptics may argue that most southern school systems, like Louisville's, had federal court–ordered desegregation plans in effect. This was true, but because these systems were often county-wide (Big Boxes), they typically linked city and suburb. Middle-class Whites could not flee to little boxes school systems. Desegregation within such Big Box systems was more successful and more stable than in areas where school desegregation plans applied solely to an inner-city school system. Such limited school desegregation efforts often helped spur White flight to private schools or to suburban little boxes systems.

During the 1970s and 1980s, southern schools were much less segregated than southern neighborhoods. (Northern school enrollments generally mirrored housing patterns closely.) During the 1990s and 2000s, however, an increasingly conservative federal judiciary, filled with over two decades of Republican appointees, accelerated the systematic dismantling of southern (and northern) desegregation orders. As a result, while residential segregation of African Americans diminished, segregation of their children in-

TABLE 1.18
LITTLE BOXES SCHOOL DISTRICTS FOSTER SEGREGATION;
BIG BOX SCHOOL DISTRICTS FACILITATE INTEGRATION

Metro area (as defined for 2000 census)	Percentage of metro area students enrolled in city schools, 1999–2000	Number of suburban school districts, 1999–2000	Black school segregation index, 1999–2000	Economic school segregation index, 1999–2000
Houston	28	42	70	55
Detroit	25	102	89	64
Columbus	27	50	70	52
Cleveland	23	84	81	62
Nashville	34	8	56	n.a.
Louisville	61	12	45	40
Indianapolis	17	52	67	46
Milwaukee	48	37	78	64
Albuquerque	73	6	36	50
Syracuse	18	35	74	42
Madison	34	15	57	32
Harrisburg	9	30	76	45
Raleigh	41	6	38	35
Richmond	16	16	61	55
Charlotte	44	10	46	34
Grand Rapids	19	62	73	46

Note: n.a. = not applicable.

creased in the public schools. Greater segregation of Black pupils and Hispanic pupils (driven by major immigration) increased the level of economic school segregation.

Lesson 22: Inelastic Areas Were Harder Hit by Deindustrialization of the American Labor Market

I certainly would not argue that major economic changes are driven by urban development patterns. The deindustrialization of the American workforce, for example, was the result primarily of global competition and technological change in manufacturing in recent decades, not of the ways in which metro areas have developed.

Deindustrialization has affected urban areas very differently. Table 1.19 shows these effects during the past four decades (when deindustrialization had already begun from America's postwar peak). The table is split into two periods: 1969–2000, which illustrates long-term trends but ends with the sustained prosperity of the mid-to-late-1990s; and 2001–09, in which a mild 2001–02 recession was followed by a period of weak recovery (2003–07) that ushered in the most severe economic crisis since the Great Depression.

Inelastic cities reached maturity during the Industrial Age. In 1969, their metro areas were still more highly industrialized (28 percent) than were elastic metro areas (19 percent), though their percentage of factory jobs had declined slightly from 35 percent in 1950. Moreover, their industrial bases (particularly Detroit's, Cleveland's, and Milwaukee's) emphasized "smokestack industries"—steel, automobiles, and other metal trades. These industries were among those hardest hit by international competition. In these three decades, the loss of manufacturing jobs was catastrophic for Detroit, Cleveland, Syracuse, and Louisville.

Several elastic areas (Albuquerque, Madison, and Raleigh) grew up largely during the postindustrial era. New export products such as computers and electronic components often characterized these metro areas' industrial activities. Important also was manufacturing of nondurable products (such as bread, dairy products, and printing), which served a growing regional population. Albuquerque, Madison, and Raleigh built impressively on small manufacturing bases. Yet manufacturing declined in importance in each of these elastic areas from 1969 to 2000.

Nevertheless, there are exceptions to these patterns. In these three decades, elastic Charlotte saw the decimation of its textile industry (–9 percent), while inelastic Grand Rapids expanded factory employment (+38 percent) in office furniture and a wide range of diversified products.

Examining metro areas within the same region or state is instructive. It minimizes Sun Belt–Frost Belt confusion. For example, while inelastic Louisville lost −24 percent of its industrial jobs, elastic

TABLE 1.19
INELASTIC REGIONS WERE HARDER HIT BY
DEINDUSTRIALIZATION OF AMERICAN LABOR MARKET

Metro area	Manufacturing jobs as percentage of total jobs, 1969	Percentage change in number of manufacturing jobs		Manufacturing jobs as percentage of total jobs, 2009
		1969–2000	2001–09	
All metro areas	23	−12	−27	7
Houston	16	+50	−2	7
Detroit	34	−26	−48	9
Columbus	23	−9	−29	6
Cleveland	33	−40	−33	10
Nashville	21	+33	−27	7
Louisville	29	−24	−28	9
Indianapolis	26	−13	−22	8
Milwaukee	33	−18	−25	12
Albuquerque	7	+191	−30	4
Syracuse	25	−32	−30	8
Madison	12	+89	−17	7
Harrisburg	19	−16	−28	6
Raleigh	15	+71	−18	5
Richmond	19	−6	−37	5
Charlotte	34	−9	−34	7
Grand Rapids	32	+38	−32	13

Nashville gained +33 percent; while inelastic Richmond lost −6 percent of its industrial jobs, elastic Raleigh gained +71 percent. More striking are the contrasts between areas that have both been caught up by deindustrialization. Both Columbus and Cleveland lost many manufacturing jobs, but elastic Columbus (both a state capital and a college town) boomed while inelastic Cleveland stagnated. The percentage decline in manufacturing jobs was also greater in inelastic Milwaukee than in elastic Indianapolis (another state capital).

During the 2000s, factory jobs took a double-digit beating everywhere but Houston. By 2009, manufacturing employment in all these target regions basically clustered around the national metropolitan average of 7 percent. Undoubtedly, the slow recovery under way will restore some manufacturing employment, but factory jobs will never play the pivotal economic role that they did a half-century ago.

Lesson 23: Elastic Areas Had Faster Rates of Nonfactory Job Creation Than Did Inelastic Areas

Whatever the trends in manufacturing, elastic areas had much greater rates of nonfactory job creation than did inelastic areas (Table 1.20). Over the first three decades, all the elastic regions doubled or even tripled their nonfactory job supply. Inelastic areas also experienced net nonfactory job growth. During the troubled 2000s, the rate of nonfactory job creation of elastic regions substantially outstripped the rate of nonfactory job creation of inelastic regions as well (though at a greatly reduced rate).

Lesson 24: Elastic Areas Showed Greater Real Income Gains Than Inelastic Areas

Job growth can be just a proxy for population growth. Did the standard of living of elastic area residents get better compared with that of inelastic area residents? The answer was *yes*, although not as dramatically as the differential in employment growth. From 1949 to 2009, real median family income (that is, adjusted for inflation) in these elastic areas as a group grew 124 percent compared with an average of 104 percent in inelastic areas (Table 1.21).

More striking was the disparity among central cities. Real median family income in the elastic cities as a group increased more than three times as much as real median family income in the inelastic cities as a group (97 percent to 30 percent, respectively). In fact, such was the degree of the flight of middle-class families from the most inelastic cities that Cleveland, Syracuse, and Harrisburg saw minimal increase in the median standard of living, and the median family in the city of Detroit was actually poorer in 2009 than it had been 60 years before!

Table 1.20

Elastic Areas Had Faster Rates of Nonfactory Job Creation Than Had Inelastic Areas

Metro area	Percentage growth in nonmanufacturing jobs	
	1969–2000	2001–09
All metro areas	116	9
Houston	211	21
Detroit	70	−5
Columbus	148	6
Cleveland	53	−1
Nashville	177	13
Louisville	98	6
Indianapolis	124	7
Milwaukee	86	3
Albuquerque	202	12
Syracuse	62	4
Madison	126	11
Harrisburg	104	6
Raleigh	262	23
Richmond	115	9
Charlotte	217	19
Grand Rapids	154	4

Lesson 25: Elastic Cities Have Better Bond Ratings Than Inelastic Cities

What were the fiscal consequences of these demographic, social, and economic patterns? Bond rating agencies must assess the risk associated with a city government's debts. Ratings are based on

TABLE 1.21

ELASTIC AREAS SHOWED GREATER REAL INCOME
GAINS THAN INELASTIC AREAS

Metro area/central city	Percentage growth in real median family income, 1949–2009	
	Metro area	Central city
Houston	100	54
Detroit	85	**-3**
Columbus	95	60
Cleveland	77	8
Nashville	141	155
Louisville (to 2000)	124	67
Louisville–Jefferson County	107	92
Indianapolis	100	66
Milwaukee	94	23
Albuquerque	97	86
Syracuse	100	19
Madison	136	108
Harrisburg	134	20
Raleigh	216	143
Richmond	132	64
Charlotte	124	110
Grand Rapids	85	41

Note: **Bold** indicates negative growth.

long-term economic outlook and past debt management. The highest rating (Aaa) indicates a blue-chip investment. A rating of Ba or lower indicates a "junk bond," which typically cannot be purchased by pension funds and other institutional investors.

The debt management of some inelastic cities (for example, Milwaukee or Grand Rapids) was better than their socioeconomic profile (Table 1.22), but the pattern of the superiority of elastic cities over inelastic cities held. Elastic cities averaged ratings better than Aa1. Inelastic cities averaged ratings slightly above A3 (discounting now-elastic Louisville–Jefferson County); more than a full rating point lower, that meant these cities paid hundreds of millions of dollars in

TABLE 1.22
ELASTIC CITIES HAVE BETTER BOND RATINGS
THAN HAVE INELASTIC CITIES

Central city	City bond rating[a]
Houston	Aa2
Detroit	Ba3
Columbus	Aaa
Cleveland	A1
Nashville	Aa1
Louisville (to 2000)	Aa2
Indianapolis	Aa1
Milwaukee	Aa2
Albuquerque	Aa1
Syracuse	A1
Madison	Aaa
Harrisburg	Ba2
Raleigh	Aaa
Richmond	Aa2
Charlotte	Aaa
Grand Rapids	Aa3

a. As of early 2012.

higher interest rates (or paid slightly less in premiums to municipal bond insurers to allow their bonds to be marketed as Aaa rated).

Lesson 26: Elastic Areas Have a Higher-Educated Workforce Than Inelastic Areas

Past prosperity may have lulled old industrial areas into complacency. Many failed to tool up for economic change. Also, in the old economy, workers moved to jobs. In the new economy, highly educated, creative people increasingly choose where they want to live depending on regional lifestyle, and then jobs tend to move to where the creative people are located.

The workforce's education level was a good measure of adaptability of areas to the postindustrial Information Age. A key measure of the workforce quality is the percentage of highly educated workers. Table 1.23 shows that elastic regions consistently had higher proportions of college-educated workers than inelastic regions. The gap was particularly notable for Albuquerque, Madison, and Raleigh—locations of both major universities and concentrations of high-tech industries—which had the highest proportions of workers with graduate and professional degrees.

Having a highly educated labor force was both consequence and cause of having a high-tech economy. Indeed, the presence of a major, high-quality university was often an engine supporting local postindustrial growth. Between our two sample groups, the major universities in elastic areas were Houston–Rice, Ohio State, Vanderbilt, Indiana–Purdue (Indianapolis campus), New Mexico, Wisconsin, and the Research Triangle's Duke–North Carolina–North Carolina State. Major universities in inelastic areas were Wayne State, Cleveland State–Case Western Reserve, Louisville, Marquette–Wisconsin (Milwaukee campus), Syracuse, Dickinson College, and Virginia Commonwealth–Richmond.[17]

With their more highly skilled labor forces and healthier central cities as living environments, elastic areas are better positioned for future economic growth in the Information Age.

Conclusion

Looking back over all the lessons, what composite profile can be drawn for inelastic and elastic areas?

TABLE 1.23
ELASTIC AREAS HAVE A HIGHER-EDUCATED WORK FORCE
THAN HAVE INELASTIC AREAS

Metro area	Percentage of area workers with bachelor's degree, 2010	Percentage of area workers with graduate or professional degree, 2010
Houston	18.6	9.5
Detroit	16.1	10.1
Columbus	21.3	10.9
Cleveland	16.3	10.0
Nashville	19.7	9.6
Louisville	14.5	9.3
Indianapolis	19.9	10.3
Milwaukee	20.3	10.2
Albuquerque	16.8	12.6
Syracuse	16.0	11.7
Madison	24.8	15.8
Harrisburg	17.6	9.9
Raleigh	27.7	13.6
Richmond	19.9	10.8
Charlotte	22.1	9.7
Grand Rapids	17.3	8.7

An inelastic area has a central city frozen within its city limits and surrounded by growing suburbs. It may have a strong downtown business district as a regional employment center, but most city neighborhoods are increasingly catch basins for poor Blacks and Hispanics. With the flight of middle-class families, the city's population has dropped steadily (typically by 20 percent or more). The income gap between city residents and suburbanites is wide and typically widening. City government is squeezed between rising service needs and eroding incomes. Unable to tap the areas of greater economic growth (its suburbs), the city becomes increasingly reliant on federal and state aid. The suburbs are typically fragmented into multiple towns and small cities and mini school systems. This very fragmentation of local government reinforces racial and economic segregation. Rivalry among jurisdictions often inhibits the whole area's ability to respond to economic challenges.

In an elastic area, suburban subdivisions expand around the central city, but the central city is able to expand as well and capture much of that suburban growth within its municipal boundaries. Although no community is free of racial inequities, minorities are more evenly spread throughout the area. Segregation by race and income class is reduced. City incomes are typically closer to (or sometimes higher than) suburban incomes. Tapping a broader tax base, an elastic city government is better financed and more inclined to rely on local resources to address local problems. In fact, local public institutions, in general, tend to be more unified and to promote more united and effective responses to economic challenges.

Did the past two decades change this picture? Major Hispanic immigration slowed (or even reversed) some inelastic cities' population decline (see Box 1.9). Young professionals and empty nesters moving back to some regentrifying city neighborhoods, coupled with the steady movement of lower-income families to some older, inner suburbs, slowed down (or even slightly reversed) the city–suburb income gap. Several inelastic cities were no longer plummeting downward, but the racial and economic chasms between inelastic cities and their suburbs remained profound. Elastic cities (and their regions) remained much better positioned for future progress.

Notes

1. By 2010, the original 168 metro areas—much expanded both in geography and population—contained three-quarters of the U.S. metropolitan population, but 67 percent now lived in their suburbs rather than in their central cities.

2. In the 98 largest metro areas, from 1998 to 2006, the proportion of jobs located within the downtown area and adjacent city neighborhoods (a 3-mile radius) decreased from 23.3 percent to 21.3 percent; the proportion of jobs located within outlying city neighborhoods and inner suburbs (a 3- to 10-mile doughnut) decreased from 34.2 percent to 33.6 percent; and by contrast, the proportion of jobs located in outer suburbs (i.e., more than 10 miles from downtown) increased from 42.5 percent to 45.1 percent. See Elizabeth Kneebone, "Job Sprawl Revisited: The Changing Geography of Metropolitan Employment," (Metro Economy Series for the Metropolitan Policy Program, Brookings Institution, Washington, DC, 2009). Because the 3-mile core encloses 28 square miles,

the 10-mile ring encloses 314 square miles, and the area of the average size of the 105 central cities in the Brookings survey is 148 square miles, well over half of all jobs must be located beyond central city boundaries.

3.   The 1950 census did not identify Hispanics as either a racial or an ethnic group (aside from about 600,000 foreign-born Hispanics of Mexican and other Latin American origin). I have adopted an estimate of about 4 million Hispanics in 1950.

Box 1.9 Immigration: Friend or Foe?

Over the past decade, Hispanic and Asian population growth accounted for 71 percent of the approximate 27 million increase in U.S. population. Despite differing opinions on the controversial topic of immigration, for inelastic cities seeking to reverse decades of continuous population decline, immigration is not their foe. In fact, it is their biggest ally.

With almost 7.9 million people, New York City had reached its peak population in 1950 and then began declining steadily, losing 800,000 residents by 1980. Seemingly miraculously, in the 1980s, New York City started to make its comeback. In the past three decades, it has gained more than 1.1 million residents to reach an all-time high.

Likewise, San Francisco had also reached its peak population of 775,000 in 1950 and lost almost 100,000 people in the next three decades. From 1980 to 2010, it more than bounced back in terms of overall population, reaching a new peak of 805,000 in 2010.

What has brought these cities back from such population decline? One key factor explains this phenomenon: immigration.

Of the approximately 1.1 million increase in New York City's population, the number of Whites and Blacks not only did not add to this increase but substantially subtracted from it. Over these past three decades, the White population dropped by almost half a million. The number of Blacks has also contributed slightly to the decline with almost 13,600 (net) leaving the city. In contrast, more than 500,000 Asians and almost 600,000 Hispanics have staked a claim and reversed New York City's dwindling population. In other words, Asian and Hispanic immigration, including the growth of second- and third-generation immigrant families, wholly accounts for the city's population rebound.

Despite San Francisco's image of trendy gentrification, the city's White population has been basically stable while the Black population has declined by 30,000. However, a net increase of almost 60,000 Asians and 25,000 Hispanics has brought San Francisco back

4.   In 2010, a majority of all Blacks as well as majorities of all Hispanics and Asians lived in metropolitan New York, NY–NJ–PA; Atlanta; Chicago, IL–IN–WI; Washington, DC–VA–MD–WV; Philadelphia, PA–NJ–DE–MD; Miami–Ft. Lauderdale; Houston; Detroit; Los Angeles–Orange County; Dallas–Ft. Worth; Baltimore; Memphis; St. Louis; Norfolk–Virginia Beach–Newport News, VA–NC; Charlotte; Cleveland; New Orleans; Richmond; San Francisco–Oakland; Orlando; Birmingham; and Tampa–St. Petersburg. Actually, if one in-

---

from its population decline. Likewise, in Chicago, the increase in Hispanic and Asian residents, many of whom were new immigrants, accounted for more than three times its net population rebound.

Overwhelmingly, immigration, not gentrification, is reversing some inelastic cities' population losses in the past three decades.[a] Ironically, the Immigration and Naturalization Act of 1965 (raising annual ceilings and eliminating a system of discriminatory national origin quotas[b]) was probably the Great Society's most successful "urban policy."

—Ashley Engel

a. Are there inelastic cities whose population gain is driven by largely White gentrification? Just a few. White gentrification has spurred a surprising population growth in Washington, D.C., for example. Washington, D.C., hit its peak population in 1950 with 806,000 people. However, by 2000, its population had dropped to 572,000. Within this past decade, this zero-elasticity city has increased by 30,000 people. Despite the loss of almost 40,000 Blacks—many of whom were middle-class Black families moving to the suburbs—D.C. has gained 6,000 Asians, almost 10,000 Hispanics, and most significantly, more than 50,000 Whites.

b. The 1965 law, in effect, nullified the Immigration Act of 1924, which was passed in nativist reaction to the massive immigration (averaging 1 million a year) that had occurred in the decade before World War I. The 1924 law capped immigration at 150,000 a year on the basis of a system of national quotas. The quotas were calculated on the basis of national origin of Americans in the *1890* census (carefully chosen to keep the door open for future immigrants from Northern Europe while slamming the door shut on potential immigrants from Eastern and Southern Europe, Asia, and, of course, Africa, whose millions of African American descendants were not accorded any "national origin" at all). In the spirit of the Monroe Doctrine, Latin Americans were not subject to national quotas, but other tools were found to discourage their entry as permanent residents.

serts Riverside–San Bernardino into the list, a majority of Hispanics lived in just seven MSAs. If San Jose, Seattle, San Diego, and Boston are inserted, a majority of Asians lived in just 10 MSAs.

5.   The eight urbanized areas where both density and Hispanic population increased were four located in California (Los Angeles–Long Beach, San Diego, San Jose, and Riverside–San Bernardino); two in Texas (Houston and Galveston–Texas City); Miami–Hialeah, FL; and Salt Lake City, UT. Small density increases in Atlantic City, NJ, and Sioux City, IA–NE–SD, may reflect simply changes in Census Bureau methodology for calculating urbanized areas.

6.   The exceptions were Santa Monica, a high-end beach community in Southern California, and Edison Township, a booming suburban job center in North Jersey.

7.   Of 684 once or current central cities for which population density for both 1950 and 2010 can be calculated, density increased in 187 cities (or 27.4 percent) and decreased in 497 cities (or 72.6 percent). Only 12 cities that increased their density were above the national average density for central cities in 1950 (6,769 persons per square mile). The 174 low-density cities averaged 2,163 persons per square mile in 1950 (one-third of the national urban average). In fact, 46 future cities had fewer than 1,000 residents per square mile and would not even have met the minimum standard for being urbanized. Two-thirds of these were rural New England towns or midwestern townships on the metropolitan fringes; one-third were southern and western cities that had recently annexed large amounts of land that was still undeveloped.

8.   In 1950, 42 future central cities were too small (such as Jonesboro and Rogers, Arkansas, or Myrtle Beach, South Carolina) for the census to report municipal area, and another 47 did not yet even exist as municipalities (such as Paradise, Lancaster, Irvine, Palm Desert, and Temecula, California, or Cape Coral and Port Saint Lucie, Florida).

9.   The designation of "elastic" or "inelastic" is always based on the characteristics of a central city. Although a metro area is also referred to as an elastic area or inelastic area, that qualifier reflects its central city's status.

10.   Albuquerque is an excellent example of this phenomenon. In 1940, Albuquerque packed 35,499 residents into its 3 square miles (a density of about 12,000 persons per square mile). With the end of World War II, however, the city fathers annexed almost 30,000 acres of undeveloped land on the slopes leading eastward toward the foothills of the Sandia Mountains. Although by 1950 Albuquerque's population had almost tripled (to 96,815), it still had thousands of acres of undeveloped land within its new city limits, enclosing 47.9 square miles. The city's population could still grow substantially even if it never added another acre. (In fact, Albuquerque's current municipal territory covers 187.7 square miles, including 22 square miles of completely undeveloped land south of the airport.)

11.   Uniquely, Nebraska state law allows a "metropolitan class city" to annex unilaterally a contiguous city of fewer than 10,000 residents. In early 2005, the city of Elkhorn (7,779 residents in 2003) surreptitiously sought to annex sev-

eral thousand acres that (a) would have raised Elkhorn's population above the 10,000 mark, forestalling any future annexation by the city of Omaha (399,357 in 2003), and (b) would have shut off Omaha's westward expansion, its only available growth path. With the support of the state courts, Omaha responded first by annexing the disputed land that would extend its city limits to be contiguous with Elkhorn's and second by annexing Elkhorn outright.

12. For somewhat different metro configurations and calculated for only a handful of metro areas, in 1970 the Black segregation index was Houston (78) and Detroit (88); Columbus (82) and Cleveland (91); Indianapolis (82) and Milwaukee (91); and Louisville (82), Richmond (77), and Charlotte (67).

13. This economic segregation index combines two calculations: based on family income, a dissimilarity index measuring the degree to which the lowest 10 percent of families (the poor) are segregated from everyone else (that is, the nonpoor) plus a separate dissimilarity index measuring the degree to which the highest 10 percent of families (the affluent) are segregated from everyone else (that is, the nonaffluent).

14. A median is the midpoint that divides a population into equal halves.

15. National Association of Home Builders (NAHB), *Smart Growth: Building Better Places to Live, Work, and Play* (Washington, DC: NAHB, 2000), 8.

16. Because the school data sources have not been updated since 1999–2000, I have not been able to update this table to 2009–10.

17. In 1950, both Charlotte and Grand Rapids lacked a major university. This gap was subsequently remedied by their respective state legislature's creation and support of the University of North Carolina at Charlotte and Grand Valley State University (both with about 25,000 students in 2011–12).

Chapter 2

Characteristics of Metropolitan Areas

How does this concept of city elasticity affect demographic, social, and economic patterns of all cities and metro areas beyond the 16 examined in Chapter 1? To analyze this phenomenon, I have constructed an "elasticity score" for as many of 786 once or current central cities in the nation's 383 metropolitan statistical areas (MSAs) as was possible.[1]

In 2010, the 383 metro areas ranged in population from Los Angeles (9,818,605) to Carson City, Nevada (55,274). Lumping regions of such disparate size into common categories produces "averages" that hide more than they reveal. Therefore, I exclude from further discussion the lowest end of the scale—the 220 metro areas with fewer than 350,000 residents in 2010.[2]

Of the 163 remaining metro areas, two other groups seem to march to a different drummer. For the following reasons, they also are excluded from my analysis. (See Box 2.1 for a third grouping whose raison d'être has vanished in recent decades.)

First, I exclude three Mexican border towns: El Paso, McAllen–Edinburg–Mission, and Brownsville–Harlingen. Along with Laredo, a smaller metro area, these Texas communities sit on the northern bank of the Rio Grande opposite major Mexican communities. With high resident populations of Hispanics (82 percent to 91 percent), hundreds of thousands living in shantytown *colonias* outside the cities' borders, and tens of thousands of Mexican workers and shoppers commuting daily across the border, these Texas metro areas are really economic and sociological extensions of northern Mexico.

The second group—"cityless metro areas"—is set apart for a purely technical reason. This group is composed of the three larger metro areas that the federal government has designated without central cities within their boundaries. All are subunits, or "metro-

Box 2.1 "White America" Vanishes

For the first edition of *Cities without Suburbs*, I excluded from my basic analysis a category of large metro areas I dubbed "White America." In 1990, these 13 large areas (Salt Lake City–Ogden and Provo–Orem, Utah; Spokane and Vancouver, Washington; Salem and Eugene–Springfield, Oregon; Boise, Idaho; Springfield, Missouri; Portland, Maine; Binghamton, New York; Manchester–Nashua, New Hampshire; Portsmouth–Dover–Rochester, New Hampshire; and Appleton–Neenah–Oshkosh, Wisconsin) had few Hispanics (2.4 percent) and fewer Blacks (0.9 percent).[a]

Of course, White America was not discrimination-free. Its small Black and Hispanic communities seemed to be exposed to "only" moderate levels of residential and school segregation.

Interestingly, however, none of its central cities had developed a significant income gap with its suburbs. City-to-suburb income percentages ranged from a low of 84 percent in Springfield, Oregon, to a high of 119 percent in Boise City, Idaho. The group's average city-to-suburb income was 98 percent—basically, parity. The very absence of city–suburb income gaps suggests the role that racial issues play as drivers of urban growth patterns and city–suburb disparities in more racially and ethnically diverse metro areas.

By 2010, however, the continued growth and spread of Hispanics around the country had mooted my earlier guidelines for defining White America (less than 2 percent Black and less than 5 percent Hispanic). Whereas the original group's percentage of Blacks had increased over two decades from 0.9 percent to only 1.4 percent, the percentage of Hispanics had tripled (from 2.4 percent to 7.8 percent). In fact, the former "capital" of White America, the Salt Lake City region, now had almost 17 percent Hispanic population.

As an indicator of these 13 regions' growing racial and ethnic diversity, an incipient city-to-suburb income gap (98 percent in 1990 to 91 percent in 2010) existed, because most of the increased lower-income Hispanic population settled in central cities.

With only 4 of the 13 metro areas still falling below my definitional thresholds, maintaining a separate category for so few White America regions (whose capital would now be Portland, Maine) hardly seemed worthwhile. In all probability, in another decade no White America regions whatsoever will exist.

a. For my basic analysis in the first edition of *Cities without Suburbs*, I defined large metro areas as those having more than 250,000 people and having a central city exceeding 100,000 people. Three dozen smaller metro areas would have also qualified as White America at that time.

politan divisions," of giant MSAs. They are Nassau County–Suffolk County, New York (i.e., Long Island); Lake County, Illinois–Kenosha County, Wisconsin; and Rockingham County–Stafford County, New Hampshire. Within these metro areas, employment locations are highly dispersed; their real central cities, of course, are respectively New York City, Chicago, and Boston. The fourth cityless metro area is Honolulu, Hawaii. Since 1907, the island of Oahu (Honolulu County) has been governed by a consolidated government. The "city" of Honolulu is only a census-designated place and has never had a separate corporate existence whose growth can be meaningfully tracked.

After excluding all of these exceptions, I have 156 metro areas for further categorization. To cut down the variation further, I have separated 16 large metro areas with principal central cities under 100,000 residents from those metro areas with principal central cities over 100,000 residents.[3] Finally, three large metro areas in Florida—Cape Coral (618,758), Port St. Lucie (424,107), and Palm Bay (543,376)—have central cities that were not even incorporated as cities until after 1950 (thus, mooting any 60-year trend analysis for those cities).

Among the 137 remaining major metro areas with central cities above 100,000 residents, the range of characteristics is still wide. Therefore, readers should not place too much emphasis on composite characteristics of different categories. The most telling tests of my point of view—the effects of urban elasticity and inelasticity—are comparisons of cities within the same region, state, or even metro area. (See Box 2.2 for further observations on what constitutes a central city.)

The results are summarized in Table 2.1. All 137 primary central cities are categorized by relative elasticity. The elasticity score represents the combined effect of a city's density (population per square mile) in 1950 and the degree to which the city expanded its limits between 1950 and 2010. Each city's initial density and degree of boundary expansion (by percentage and absolute area) are ranked against those of all other cities in the 163 metro areas with population above 350,000 (plus all secondary central cities with population of 100,000 or more within these 163 metro areas). A city's relative rankings (grouped into deciles) for the two key characteristics (initial density and boundary expansion) are added together to produce a composite elasticity score with the degree of boundary expansion awarded three times the weight of initial density.[4]

New York City ranks in the lowest decile (1) for having the highest population density in 1950 (25,046 per square mile). It also ranks in the lowest decile for not expanding its city limits at all. Therefore,

---

Box 2.2 How Many Central Cities?

For the 1950 census, the Census Bureau[a] designated 193 central cities for 168 metro areas. They ranged in population from New York City (7,891,957) to Ashland, Kentucky (31,131).

In the decades since, new central cities have been designated in newly recognized metro areas (that now officially total 348), and additional central cities have been added as, in effect, secondary job centers to the core city. Meanwhile, other cities have lost their designation as central cities as demographic and employment patterns—and personnel at the Census Bureau—have changed.

By my best count, between 1950 and 2010, the Census Bureau has had 802 designated central cities, including the following:

- Sixteen central cities that are not municipalities at all but unincorporated census-designated places. They include military bases (Fort Hood, Texas, and Fort Stewart, Georgia); giant subdivisions with big homeowners' associations (such as Reston, Virginia); an urban county that is a city in all but legal status (Arlington County, Virginia); and most notably, Honolulu, Hawaii, which, being part of a unified, island-wide City and County of Honolulu since 1907, has never had a separate municipal existence.
- Nine central cities that have been downgraded from metropolitan to micropolitan status. They include Los Alamos, New Mexico; Gettysburg, Pennsylvania; and most regrettably, Midland, Michigan.
- Forty-five central cities that were incorporated as municipalities after 1950, the starting date of my analysis. All but 2 are located in Big Box regions, with 9 new cities in Florida and 19 in California. Included are some sizable cities, such as Scottsdale, Arizona (217,385); Overland Park, Kansas (173,372); Port St. Lucie (164,603) and Palm Bay (103,190), Florida; and Fremont (214,089), Irvine (212,375), Lancaster (156,633), Thousand Oaks (126,683), Victorville (115,903), Carlsbad (105,328), and Temecula (100,097), California—certainly illustrating the Sun Belt's explosive growth.

New York City's elasticity score is the minimum 4 [1 + (3 × 1)]. Anchorage ranks in the highest decile (10) for having among the lowest population densities in 1950 (900 per square mile). It ranks in the highest decile for having one of the highest boundary expansion rates (13,482 percent). Therefore, Anchorage's elasticity score is the maximum 40 [10 + (3 × 10)].

- Forty-two central cities that were too small in 1950 (fewer than 2,500 residents) to have their municipal area reported by the Census Bureau. I also have been unable to locate the information for those cities.

After Census 2000, the Census Bureau and Office of Management and Budget went wild in their designations. Not only did they add 217 counties to 118 existing metro areas (an unprecedented, post-census expansion), but they also created 49 new metro areas composed of 81 counties.

More troublesome, however, was the proliferation of designated "principal cities" in some metro areas. An extreme example is the Los Angeles metro division, composed solely of massive Los Angeles County. In 1950, Los Angeles was the only designated central city. For the 1960, 1970, and 1980 censuses, Los Angeles was joined by Long Beach. Pasadena, Burbank, and Pomona were added for 1990. Burbank and Pomona were de-designated, but Lancaster was added for Census 2000. Then, for Census 2010, Burbank and Pomona were redesignated (though Lancaster was demoted), and 11 new principal cities were designated (averaging only 87,000 people).

Whatever the role that these secondary suburban job centers play, putting a Cerritos (49,041) on a par with Los Angeles (3,792,621) — or even Long Beach (462,257) — is ridiculous.

Thus, in calculations such as city-to-suburban per capita income percentage or city-to-suburban minority ratio, I treat only the historic central cities (Los Angeles and Long Beach, in this case) as the cities and place other designated "principal cities" in the "suburban" column.

a. In actuality, since the 1970s, the official designating authority has been the federal Office of Management and Budget within the Executive Office of the President. Throughout this book I adopt the convention that metro areas, central cities, and so on are determined by the Census Bureau because it was (and continues to be) the primary source of analysis and implementer of the system.

I have ranked all cities by their elasticity scores and split them into five groupings: zero elasticity, low elasticity, medium elasticity, high elasticity, and hyper elasticity. These 137 largest metro areas are ranked in ascending order of elasticity in Table 2.1. (New York City is at the lowest of the zero-elasticity group; Anchorage leads the hyper-elasticity group.)

TABLE 2.1

137 MAJOR METRO AREAS GROUPED BY PRINCIPAL CENTRAL CITY'S ELASTICITY

Zero elasticity (31 areas)	Elasticity score	Low elasticity (27 areas)	Elasticity score	Medium elasticity (28 areas)	Elasticity score	High elasticity (26 areas)	Elasticity score	Hyper elasticity (25 areas)	Elasticity score
New York, NY	4.0	New Orleans, LA	11.5	Portland, OR	23.0	Savannah, GA	27.0	Albuquerque, NM	31.5
Washington, DC	4.0	Cincinnati, OH	11.5	Salinas, CA[a]	23.0	Springfield, MO[a]	27.0	Corpus Christi, TX	31.5
Detroit, MI	4.0	Oakland, CA	12.0	Denver, CO	23.5	Memphis, TN	28.0	San Antonio, TX	32.0
Minneapolis, MN	5.0	Albany, NY	12.0	Omaha, NE	23.5	Charleston, SC	28.0	Fort Worth, TX	32.0
Hartford, CT	5.0	Chicago, IL	13.0	Davenport, IA	23.5	Wichita, KS	28.0	Orlando, FL	32.0
Rochester, NY	5.0	Allentown, PA	13.0	Rockford, IL	23.5	Indianapolis, IN	28.5	San Jose, CA	32.0
Boston, MA	5.5	Flint, MI	14.0	Atlanta, GA	24.0	Little Rock, AR	28.5	Raleigh, NC	32.0
St. Louis, MO	5.5	Canton, OH	15.0	Provo, UT[a]	24.0	Chattanooga, TN	28.5	Lexington, KY	32.0
Camden, NJ[a]	5.5	Manchester, NH	15.0	Salem, OR[a]	24.5	Mobile, AL	28.5	Reno, NV[a]	32.5
Paterson, NJ	5.5	Tacoma, WA	15.5	Baton Rouge, LA	25.0	Kansas City, MO	29.0	Huntsville, AL[a]	32.5
Syracuse, NY	6.0	Akron, OH	15.5	Madison, WI	25.0	Louisville, KY	29.0	Killeen, TX[a]	32.5
Providence, RI	7.0	Los Angeles, CA	16.0	Vallejo, CA[a]	25.0	Fresno, CA	29.0	Tallahassee, FL[a]	32.5
Newark, NJ	7.0	Seattle, WA	16.0	Sacramento, CA	25.5	Jackson, MS	29.0	Nashville, TN	33.0
Buffalo, NY	8.0	Milwaukee, WI	16.0	Fort Wayne, IN	25.5	Durham, NC	29.0	Bakersfield, CT[a]	33.0
Pittsburgh, PA	8.0	Norfolk, VA	16.5	Birmingham, AL	25.5	Dallas, TX	29.5	Augusta, GA	33.0
New Haven, CT	8.0	Grand Rapids, MI	16.5	Knoxville, TN	25.5	Tulsa, OK	29.5	Phoenix, AZ	34.0
Trenton, NJ	8.5	Richmond, VA	17.5	Modesto, CA[a]	25.5	Visalia, CA[a]	29.5	Austin, TX	34.0
Springfield, MA	9.5	Evansville, IN	18.0	Santa Rosa, CA[a]	25.5	Boise City, ID[a]	29.5	Jacksonville, FL	34.0
Baltimore, MD	9.5	Ann Arbor, MI[a]	18.5	Eugene, OR[a]	25.5	Anaheim, CA[a]	30.5	Oklahoma City, OK	34.5

City	Value	City	Value	City	Value	City	Value	City	Value
Cleveland, OH	9.5	Dayton, OH	18.5	Columbus, OH	26.0	San Diego, CA	30.5	Tucson, AZ[a]	34.5
Worcester, MA	9.5	Lansing, MI	19.0	West Palm Beach, FL[a]	26.0	Montgomery, AL	31.0	Colorado Springs, CO[a]	34.5
Wilmington, DE	9.5	Spokane, WA	19.0	Salt Lake City, UT	26.0	Houston, TX	31.0	Fayetteville, NC[a]	35.0
Reading, PA	10.0	Toledo, OH	19.5	Stockton, CA	26.0	Oxnard, CA[a]	31.0	Charlotte, NC	35.5
Philadelphia, PA	10.0	Gary, IN[a]	20.0	Shreveport, LA	26.0	Columbia, SC	31.0	Las Vegas, NV[a]	36.0
San Francisco, CA	10.5	Fort Lauderdale, FL[a]	21.0	Beaumont, TX	26.0	Greensboro, NC	31.0	Anchorage, AK[a]	40.0
Jersey City, NJ	10.5	Peoria, IL	21.0	Wilmington, NC[a]	26.0	Winston-Salem, NC	31.0		
Miami, FL	10.5	Des Moines, IA	21.5	Riverside, CA[a]	26.5				
Scranton, PA	11.0			Tampa, FL	26.5				
Bridgeport, CT	11.0								
Youngstown, OH	11.0								
Harrisburg, PA	11.0								

a. City not identified as a central city in the 1950 census.

The 31-member zero-elasticity group includes four inelastic cities analyzed in Chapter 1 (Detroit, Syracuse, Cleveland, and Harrisburg). This group also includes New York, Philadelphia, Baltimore, St. Louis, Buffalo, Newark, and Pittsburgh, which are often found on lists of troubled cities. In addition, the zero-elasticity group includes Boston, San Francisco, Minneapolis, and Washington, D.C.— cities seen as being in relatively good shape.

The 27-member low-elasticity group includes Milwaukee, Grand Rapids, and Richmond (discussed in Chapter 1) as well as Los Angeles, Chicago, Seattle, New Orleans, Cincinnati, Oakland, and Norfolk. It may be surprising to find Chicago edging (just barely) into the low-elasticity group. However, in the 1950s, Chicago annexed 17 square miles west of the city where O'Hare International Airport and vast office and warehouse complexes are located.

Of the cities analyzed in Chapter 1, Columbus and Madison are among the 28 medium-elasticity cities as well as Portland (Oregon), Denver, Atlanta, and Sacramento.

Houston, Indianapolis–Marion, and Louisville–Jefferson (transformed by city–county consolidation in 2003 from low elasticity to high elasticity) are among the 26 high-elasticity cities as well as San Diego, Dallas, Memphis, and Kansas City (Missouri).

Finally, the 25 hyper-elasticity cities include Albuquerque, Nashville–Davidson, Raleigh, and Charlotte (analyzed in Chapter 1), along with other major city–county consolidations (Jacksonville–Duval, Lexington–Fayette, Augusta–Richmond, and Anchorage–Anchorage Borough). The list of hyper-elasticity cities is rounded out by such annexation powerhouses as San Antonio, Fort Worth, Phoenix, San Jose, Austin, Oklahoma City, Las Vegas, and Tucson.

Table 2.2 summarizes the average population growth of the metro areas in each group. The zero-elasticity group began and ended with the largest average metro population and experienced the lowest rate of metro population growth (49 percent). The other groups doubled, tripled, or even increased almost fivefold their average populations.[5] Disparities in growth rates, however important, should not be allowed to obscure the fact that all groups, including the zero-elasticity group, added an average of 666,000 to 970,000 residents between 1950 and 2010.

What about the factors that affected different central cities' elasticity? Table 2.3 illustrates the average population density in 1950 of central cities in each group. At 12,797 persons per square mile (or 189 percent of the midcentury average for 193 central cities of 6,769 persons per square mile), zero-elasticity cities had little vacant

TABLE 2.2
ALMOST ALL METRO AREAS HAVE GROWN

Metro area	Average metro population		Percentage change	
	1950	2010	1950–2010	2000s
Zero elasticity	1,367,749	2,034,109	49	4
Low elasticity	790,144	1,564,849	98	4
Medium elasticity	330,381	1,200,546	263	17
High elasticity	391,377	1,289,712	230	15
Hyper elasticity	244,450	1,214,401	397	24

TABLE 2.3
LOW-DENSITY CITIES CAN GROW THROUGH INFILL;
HIGH-DENSITY CITIES CANNOT

Central city	Average city density (persons per square mile), 1950	Average city density as a percentage of national city average, 1950
Zero elasticity	12,797	189
Low elasticity	6,675	99
Medium elasticity	5,290	78
High elasticity	5,583	82
Hyper elasticity	4,820	71

land for new, low-density subdivision development; they had little alternative but to try to expand their boundaries. Low-elasticity cities were right at the national average density. Medium-, high-, and hyper-elasticity cities had some room to grow internally—although they would expand their boundaries dramatically as well.

Table 2.4 demonstrates that double-barreled advantage. Zero-elasticity cities barely expanded their city limits (statistically, by 1 percent); typically, they expanded through lakefront, riverfront, and bayshore reclamation (or simply from more accurate surveying). Low-elasticity cities expanded modestly (25 percent), but cities

Table 2.4
Elastic Cities Expand Their City Limits; Inelastic Cities Do Not

Central city	Average city area (square miles)			Percentage change
	1950	2010	2000s	1950–2010
Zero elasticity	48	48	0	1
Low elasticity	62	78	0	25
Medium elasticity	25	87	4	239
High elasticity	37	182	22	392
Hyper elasticity	22	325	23	1,365
Without Anchorage	23	267	23	1,084

in the medium-, high- and hyper-elasticity categories spread far and wide across the landscape, expanding 3-, 5-, and 14-fold in territory, respectively. (Setting aside Anchorage's massive, 1,686-square-mile land grab, hyper-elasticity cities still expanded almost 12-fold in land area.)

By 2010 (six decades into the Age of Sprawl), the average zero-elasticity city was the smallest in geographic area (48 square miles), although the group covered a wide range in municipal size from Trenton (7.6 square miles) to New York City (302.6 square miles). By contrast, the average hyper-elasticity city was almost eight times as large geographically (six times without counting Anchorage).

The demographic payoff is summed up in Table 2.5, which shows each group's relative capture/contribute percentage. Over the six decades, zero-elasticity cities contributed –17 percent of their regions' net population growth; in other words, these central cities provided 17 percent of their own suburbs' population growth. Low-elasticity cities essentially broke even (2 percent). Medium-elasticity cities captured a modest 15 percent, and high-elasticity cities a somewhat higher 29 percent. Hyper-elasticity cities, however, captured almost half of their regions' net population growth (43 percent). Moreover, these patterns continued in the 2000s. Zero-elasticity cities are the victims of their suburbs, but high- and hyper-elasticity cities often *are* their own suburbs.

Table 2.6 demonstrates the dramatically different consequences on the population trends among central cities. The 31 zero-elasticity

TABLE 2.5
ELASTIC CITIES *CAPTURE* SUBURBAN GROWTH;
INELASTIC CITIES *CONTRIBUTE* TO SUBURBAN GROWTH

Elasticity category	Average city capture/ contribute percentage, 1950–2010	Average city capture/ contribute percentage, 2000s
Zero elasticity	−17	−5
Without New York City	−19	−12
Low elasticity	+2	−14
Without Los Angeles	−8	−15
Medium elasticity	+15	+11
High elasticity	+29	+22
Hyper elasticity	+43	+33

TABLE 2.6
ELASTIC CITIES GAIN POPULATION; INELASTIC CITIES LOSE POPULATION

Central city	Average city population		Percentage change	
	1950	2010	1950–2010	2000s
Zero elasticity	742,426	584,248	−21	−1
Without New York City	495,890	322,494	−35	−3
Low elasticity	416,883	437,194	+5	−3
Without Los Angeles	357,134	308,139	−14	−5
Medium elasticity	134,827	261,674	+94	+8
High elasticity	180,112	441,180	+145	+10
Hyper elasticity	100,314	521,792	+420	+18

cities lost population (an average change of −21 percent) except for New York, Paterson, Miami, and San Francisco. These four cities' recent population gains were fueled entirely by Asian and Hispanic immigration. If New York City is excluded, zero-elasticity cities' population change was −35 percent.

Low-elasticity cities as a group gained 5 percent in population; that gain was largely the result of Los Angeles's being in this category. Most of these cities' annexation activities occurred in the 1950s and 1960s, and population began to fall thereafter. Of 27 low-elasticity cities, 20 lost population since their historic population peaks (including pre–Hurricane Katrina New Orleans).

Among the 28 medium-elasticity cities (which gained 94 percent in population overall), only Beaumont and Salt Lake City (minor losses both), Birmingham (major losses), and Atlanta lost population since earlier peaks; all four cities' annexations slowed in recent

---

Box 2.3 Atlanta: The Two Faces of Progress

Like San Francisco, Seattle, Boston, and Washington, D.C., Atlanta is the cultural and economic heart of a wealthy, vastly larger metropolitan area. Indeed, with the Atlanta metro area having officially grown from a three-county, 1,137-square-mile region in 1950 to a 28-county, 8,279-square-mile region in 2010, local boosters (with a touch of perverse pride) describe the Atlanta area as "the most rapidly expanding human settlement in the history of mankind."

In the 1950s, the city tripled in size from 37 square miles to 128 square miles. Its new territory embraced the North Atlanta and Buckhead areas, future home to many upper-middle-class, largely White families, and extended 7 miles south of downtown to the Hartsfield–Jackson Atlanta International Airport, the world's busiest.[a]

As measured by its city-to-suburb per capita income percentage, Atlanta's rise has been even more spectacular. In 1980, the city's per capita income was 82 percent of suburban per capita income; in 1990, 89 percent; in 2000, 104 percent; and in 2010, 133 percent! Particularly after the Atlanta Olympic Games in 1996, Atlanta became a hot spot for yuppies and buppies.

But far more White yuppies than Black buppies. In fact, in 2010, the per capita income of White city residents ($65,150) was almost four times the per capita income of Black city residents ($17,536).[b]

This gaping disparity underscores the two Atlantas: White Atlanta and Black Atlanta. Of White Atlantans, 63 percent either lived alone or with unrelated roommates. The poverty rate among the remaining 37 percent that were family households was only 2.9 percent. Even among White single mothers with children (less than 2 percent of all White households), the poverty rate was barely 20 percent. In short, most White "per capitas" were wage earners; few White dependents brought per capita incomes down (only 13 percent were children).

years. Fueled by White gentrification, however, Atlanta (which had lost more than 100,000 residents between 1970 and 1990) made a strong comeback in the past three decades (see Box 2.3).

Among the 51 high- and hyper-elasticity cities, none had a smaller population in 2010 than in 1950, and only Kansas City, Missouri, had declined slightly from an intervening peak population. (Kansas City annexed massive territory northward, leading to its international airport, but most new, middle-income subdivisions were built

---

In Black Atlanta, the proportion of those living alone or with unrelated roommates was only 49 percent (still substantial but markedly less than White Atlanta's 63 percent). The Black family poverty rate was 29.4 percent (10 times the White rate). Among Black single mothers with children (20 percent of total Black households), the poverty rate was 54 percent. In all, almost 25 percent of Black Atlantans were dependent children, and the majority were poor.

This demographic reality was reflected in the Atlanta Public Schools, which 84 percent of school-age children attended. In the most recent school year, 83 percent of Atlanta Public Schools students were Black, 10 percent White, and 7 percent Hispanic and other. More significantly, 75 percent qualified for free and reduced-price meals, with the baleful consequences that economically segregated classrooms bring (see Box 2.5).[c]

The Atlanta Housing Authority has launched a laudable campaign to replace its massive housing projects with rebuilt, mixed-income, garden apartment and townhouse complexes to reduce concentrations of poor families. Nevertheless, decade after decade, the economic gap between the two Atlantas grows.

a. With these annexations, Atlanta classifies as a medium-elasticity city, yet in the past 50 years, it has added little new territory (just 5 square miles).

b. The source of all data used in this commentary (except school data) is the five-year averages from American Community Survey 2006–10. Five-year averages greatly reduce the margin of error of the census surveys, but for these years, understate the impact of the Great Recession, which began in 2008.

c. Much heralded improvement in Atlanta Public Schools test scores vanished when, after skeptical analysis by the *Atlanta Journal-Constitution*, federal and state investigators turned up irrefutable evidence of widespread test score altering by many school principals and teachers.

south of the city in Johnson County, Kansas.) High-elasticity cities more than doubled in population (145 percent), but hyper-elasticity cities increased their number of residents fivefold (420 percent).

Of course, all such categorizations of elasticity are based on history. The fact that a central city may have annexed much of its region's new development in the past is no guarantee that it will continue to be elastic in the future. By 2010, absent major Hispanic and Asian immigration, a truth has been demonstrated many times: when a city stops growing geographically, it starts shrinking demographically.

However, let's pause to consider the issue raised in Chapter 1 and Box 1.7: differences between population trends and household trends.

Simply tracking raw population counts is misleading because in the past six decades American household structure has undergone substantial transformation. In these 137 major metro areas, the average household size was 3.5 persons in 1950; by 2010, average household size was 2.7—a 24 percent reduction. Families now have fewer children. Extended families are rare. Most elderly parents live independently, as do most young adults. In fact, although a dozen metro areas did lose population over six decades, not a single one of the 383 metro areas had fewer households in 2010 than in 1950.

What are the implications for a city? A city could lose 24 percent of its population and still contain the same number of households (read "residential taxpayers"). Compare Table 2.7 with Table 2.6. Even zero-elasticity cities as a category largely held their own with regard to number of households they contain. The big population losers still lost households, such as Pittsburgh (–29 percent change), Buffalo (–32 percent), Cleveland (–37 percent), Youngstown (–41 change), St. Louis (–45 percent), and Detroit (–47 percent). Such zero-elasticity cities were still decimated fiscally and economically. But others were relatively prosperous. Boston lost 23 percent of its population but had a 15 percent increase in number of households. The population of Washington, D.C., dropped 25 percent, but it had 19 percent more households in 2010 than in 1950.

In all, 18 of 31 zero-elasticity and 7 of 27 low-elasticity cities were net household losers, whereas none of the medium-, high- and hyper-elasticity cities (except Birmingham[6]) failed to capture a positive share of regional household growth. These 26 household-losing cities substantially constitute the list of America's most troubled major cities.[7]

Of course, highly elastic cities had correspondingly greater household growth than population growth. Although hyper-elasticity cit-

TABLE 2.7
ELASTIC CITIES GAIN MANY HOUSEHOLDS;
INELASTIC CITIES CAN LOSE HOUSEHOLDS

Elasticity category	Average city households, 1950	Average city households, 2010	Percentage change in average city households, 1950–2010	Number of cities losing households, 1950–2010
Zero elasticity	210,249	221,705	+5	18
Without New York City	140,903	128,541	–9	
Low elasticity	128,492	168,929	+31	7
Without Los Angeles	107,828	124,727	+16	
Medium elasticity	40,341	103,452	+156	1
High elasticity	54,212	168,874	+212	0
Hyper elasticity	29,026	197,644	+581	0

ies, for example, experienced a fivefold increase in population, they had an almost sevenfold increase in households.

Cities tended to capture a greater share of regional household growth than regional population growth because more single-person households were attracted to live in more urban (and more urbane) neighborhoods.[8] In contrast, certain inelastic cities with high percentages of low-income African American and Latino households often had higher household sizes than their generally White, middle-class suburbs.[9]

The social and economic consequences of these striking differences in city–suburb dynamics are illustrated in the next several tables. Table 2.8 shows that in 2010 most groups had roughly the same percentage of Blacks metro-wide (from 11 percent to 13 percent) with only the high-elasticity category (half of whose metro areas are in the South) being a statistical outlier (18 percent). The racial profile of central cities, however, differed substantially.

Because of the high concentration of Blacks within the inner city, zero-elasticity cities were 34 percent Black (over four times their suburban average of 8 percent). On a neighborhood-by-neighborhood

Table 2.8

Inelastic Areas Are More Racially Segregated
Than Are Elastic Areas

Elasticity category	Average percentage Black, 2010			Average metro segregation index,[a] 2010	Average index improvement, 1980–2010
	Metro area	City	Suburbs		
Zero elasticity	13	34	8	63	−10
Low elasticity	13	27	9	57	−12
Medium elasticity	11	20	8	48	−14
High elasticity	18	29	12	51	−14
Hyper elasticity	13	18	9	44	−13

a. Segregation index: scale 0 to 100 (100 = total apartheid); lower numbers represent improvement.

basis, the Black segregation index was a high 63 in zero-elasticity metro areas in 2010 (that is, in typically little boxes regions).

By contrast, hyper-elasticity cities embraced so much of their own suburban development that the proportion of Blacks in the city (18 percent) was not that much higher than the percentage metro-wide (13 percent) and only twice the suburban average (9 percent). On a metro-wide basis, the index of Black segregation in these Big Box regions was 44 in 2010 (significantly lower but still unacceptable).

At the peak period of residential segregation, around 1970, metro Black segregation indices typically ranged in the 70s, 80s, and even low 90s.[10] However, residential segregation of Blacks has been steadily (if too slowly) reduced in most metro areas. From 1980 to 2010, Black segregation indices fell in 132 of these 137 metro areas.[11] The rate of improvement in elastic, typically Big Box regions (13 to 14 points) was somewhat greater than it was in inelastic, typically little boxes regions (10 to 12 points). In 2010, of 41 metro areas with 1 million or more people and at least a 10 percent Black population, the most segregated metro area was Milwaukee (80); the least segregated metro area was Las Vegas (36), which over the previous three decades also had the greatest rate of improvement (63 to 36).

The New York City region showed almost no improvement at all (81.7 to 79.1).

As suggested in Chapter 1, segregation of Hispanics was primarily influenced by immigration patterns. The Hispanic population increased significantly in each of the 137 metro areas over the past three decades. The two extremes illustrate overall trends in Hispanic segregation. In 1980, metro Raleigh had only 2,995 Hispanic residents, or less than 1 percent of its population. Drawn by the region's booming job market, tens of thousands of Hispanics flocked to metro Raleigh; by 2010, metro Raleigh had 114,512 Hispanics—a growth rate of 3,723 percent, or a 38-fold increase—and Hispanics totaled over 10 percent of the regional population. With many locating in port-of-entry, increasingly Hispanic neighborhoods, the Hispanic segregation index increased from 20 to 37.

By contrast, in 1980, metro Corpus Christi already had a very large, long-established Hispanic population (158,044, or over 48 percent of its population). Both natural increase and immigration added another 89,137 Hispanics, or a 56 percent growth rate. However, without the relative influx of new immigrants, Hispanics continued to scatter across a wider range of neighborhoods, lowering the Hispanic segregation index from 52 to 42.

Metro Flint illustrates a third pattern. Like the Raleigh area, the Flint area had relatively few Hispanics in 1980 (7,649, or less than 2 percent of the population). However, unlike Raleigh, Flint's economy was declining. Though the region's Hispanic population grew to 12,983, most of the 70 percent growth came through natural increase and not immigration. Like Corpus Christi, Flint's Hispanic population steadily moved into a wider range of neighborhoods, lowering its Hispanic segregation index from 36 to 23.

These distinctions are illustrated by Table 2.9, which departs from my analysis of the impact of relative elasticity. Table 2.9 divides the 137 metro areas into six groups according to the percentage of Hispanic population in 1980 and subsequent growth rate over the three decades. With one exception, the 13 Group A members are Sun Belt regions like Raleigh that experienced explosive immigration;[12] Hispanic segregation increased by double digits. The 12 Group F members are Sun Belt regions like Corpus Christi (again, with one exception) that had major, long-established Hispanic populations.[13] The growth of their Hispanic populations was additive but not transformative. Segregation indices decreased in half and increased only slightly in the other half. A majority of the 25 members of Group C were (like Flint) largely declining midwestern industrial regions.[14]

TABLE 2.9
MAJOR IMMIGRATION INCREASES HISPANIC SEGREGATION

Metro area by Hispanic population, 1980	Growth in percentage of Hispanic population, 1980–2010	Average Hispanic segregation index[a]		Average change in Hispanic segregation index,[a] 1980–2010
		1980	2000	
A. Less than 5 percent Hispanic; explosive growth (13 members)	1,015 to 3,723	24.4	43.2	+18.8
B. Less than 5 percent Hispanic; rapid growth (59 members)	301 to 988	34.9	41.7	+6.8
C. Less than 5 percent Hispanic; modest growth (25 members)	70 to 299	39.1	37.4	−1.7
D. 5 percent to 10 percent Hispanic; modest growth (13 members)	113 to 1521	45.9	46.5	+0.6
Without Las Vegas	113 to 629	47.9	46.9	−1.0
E. 10 percent to 20 percent Hispanic; modest growth (15 members)	78 to 589	42.0	44.7	+1.5
F. More than 20 percent Hispanic; modest growth (12 members)	56 to 374	51.0	48.4	−2.6

a. Segregation index: scale 0 to 100 (100 = total apartheid); lower numbers represent improvement.

TABLE 2.10
HIGHLY RACIALLY SEGREGATED REGIONS
ARE HIGHLY ECONOMICALLY SEGREGATED REGIONS

Metro area	Average metro economic segregation index[a]				
	1969	1979	1989	1999	2009
Zero elasticity	29	30	37	36	39
Low elasticity	26	27	35	33	35
Medium elasticity	26	24	30	29	32
High elasticity	31	28	34	32	35
Hyper elasticity	30	27	33	32	34

a. Segregation index: scale 0 to 100 (100 = total apartheid); lower numbers represent improvement.

To characterize the population group's doubling, tripling, quadrupling, and so on as only "moderate" growth underscores the phenomenal increase in the nation's Hispanic population, the most significant demographic trend of the past 30 years.

The analysis of *economic* disparities returns to the relative elasticity format in Table 2.10.[15] Highly racially segregated regions are highly economically segregated regions. Contrary to the trends for Black segregation, between 1970 and 2010 economic segregation increased in 121 of 134 metro areas for which data were available. With the sole exception of zero-elasticity Wilmington, Delaware (where economic segregation declined almost imperceptibly from 35.5 to 35.3), the other dozen regions where economic segregation decreased were all medium-, high- and hyper-elasticity regions in the South.[16] Jim Crow by income is replacing Jim Crow by race (except, ironically, in some southern regions).

Table 2.11 analyzes patterns in income among the elasticity groups. Sixty years ago, median family incomes in central cities equaled or exceeded median family incomes for the entire regions. A rough parity existed between city and suburban incomes. Thereafter, in the Age of Sprawl, central city incomes dropped below metro-wide medians. For zero-elasticity cities, the decline was precipitous; they plummeted 34 percentage points to only 62 percent of the region-wide median by 2009. For hyper-elasticity cities that incorporated so many of their suburbs within their expanding city limits, the relative decline was much less; they slid only 13 percentage points to 94 percent of the region-wide median family income in 2009.

Table 2.11
Inelastic Cities Have Wide Income Gaps with Suburbs;
Elastic Cities Maintain Greater City–Suburb Balance

Central city	City percentage of metro median family income		City percentage of suburban per capita income	
	1949	2005–09	1979	2005–09
Zero elasticity	96	62	74	65
Low elasticity	101	76	89	81
Medium elasticity	106	87	96	91
High elasticity	106	90	102	94
Hyper elasticity	107	94	105	97

The growing economic imbalance between cities and suburbs is reinforced by contrasting per capita income levels in central cities with suburban per capita income levels. By 1979, zero-elasticity cities' per capita incomes had fallen to 74 percent of suburban levels. Despite the media-touted comeback of many older central cities, the city-to-suburb income gap for all categories of cities widened over the next three decades. Zero-elasticity cities dropped to 65 percent in 2009. By contrast, hyper-elasticity cities had maintained rough income parity with their suburbs up to 1979 (105 percent) and largely held that position of parity in 2009 (97 percent).

Another critical measure of the economic health of central cities is the "fair share of poverty index" (Table 2.12).[17] In 2009, poverty was much more concentrated in inelastic cities than in elastic cities. Inelastic cities were cast in the role of home for most of their metro areas' poor minorities, as clearly indicated by disparities in the central cities' fair share of poverty index. In 2009, zero-elasticity cities had more than twice the fair share of poverty (an index of 253) that hyper-elasticity cities had (118).

That disproportion was not just a temporary phenomenon during the Great Recession. Central cities' fair share of poverty index had been rising decade by decade since 1969. However, the increases were catastrophic for zero-elasticity cities (from 173 to 253) and low-elasticity cities (from 135 to 189), whereas the rise was more gradual for the more elastic cities, and the disparities were still at tolerable levels.

TABLE 2.12
POVERTY IS MORE DISPROPORTIONATELY CONCENTRATED IN INELASTIC
CITIES THAN IN ELASTIC CITIES

	Poverty rate, 2005–09		City fair share of poverty index	
Elasticity category	Metro	City	2005–09	1969
Zero elasticity	8.3	20.9	253	173
Low elasticity	8.8	16.6	189	135
Medium elasticity	9.3	13.7	147	111
High elasticity	10.9	14.2	131	113
Hyper elasticity	10.2	12.0	118	105

Moreover, elastic cities' lesser concentration of poverty by juris-diction was not just an artifact of these cities being larger propor-tions of their metro areas. As Table 2.10 shows, elastic regions also had somewhat less concentration of poverty on a neighborhood-by-neighborhood basis. By controlling planning, zoning, and housing policy for a larger portion of the region, elastic cities have the capac-ity to help spread low- and moderate-income housing across a wide range of neighborhoods.

In Chapter 1, I presented several explanations for these disparities in racial and income distribution. I now review them in the context of this broader analysis.

First, differences in racial and economic segregation are not re-lated to the proportion of Blacks or poor people in metro areas. Re-gions with high proportions of Blacks or poor people may be highly segregated or quite well integrated. Similarly, regions with low pro-portions of Blacks and poor people may find them well blended into the larger community or, conversely, highly isolated.

Second, although the proportion of minorities metro-wide seems to have little to do with the degree of racial segregation, the historic distribution, or racial profile, plays some role. Historically, many Blacks and Hispanics lived in rural and small-town areas in the South and West, but they did not live in such areas in the Northeast and Midwest. As urbanization has reached into the countryside, southern and western cities have not encountered as sharp "racial gradients" as have northeastern and midwestern cities.

Third, the absolute size of the metro area has little effect on the racial and economic isolation of city dwellers. Some of the country's largest cities and metro areas are concentrated within the zero-elasticity category, which suggests that metro and city population size is a factor. However, the relationship of population size to segregation (racial and economic) is weak.

More significant is the maturity of the city. Table 2.13 depicts the average date by which cities in each group passed the 100,000 population mark. On average, the zero-elasticity cities passed the mark in 1888, and the low-elasticity cities passed the mark in 1919. Generally, these were pre–Automobile Age cities. On average, by contrast, medium-, high-, and hyper-elasticity cities reached 100,000 residents in 1954, 1946, and 1962, respectively, within the era of the dominance of the suburban lifestyle.

A central city's age has many implications. By definition, an old city has an inventory of old, often decaying neighborhoods that typically become home to many poor people. A long-established Black or Hispanic population in an old city may have become highly isolated as victims of the social prejudices of an earlier era. Even an old city's long participation in certain social welfare programs, such as public housing, may reinforce racial and economic isolation. In any event, a city's age strongly influences racial and economic segregation within a metro area.

Finally, a central city's elasticity has the highest relationship of all these factors to the level of racial and economic segregation in a metro area. Why some central cities expanded and others did not must really be the subject of case-by-case studies. My five categories of elasticity bring together many different cities from many different regions, but some general observations can be made.

TABLE 2.13
INELASTIC CITIES ARE OLDER THAN ELASTIC CITIES

Type of city	Census when the population exceeded 100,000
Zero elasticity	1888
Low elasticity	1919
Medium elasticity	1954
High elasticity	1946
Hyper elasticity	1962

In general, state laws regarding annexation are less inhibiting in the South and West than they are in the Northeast and Midwest. Old cities (often in the Northeast and Midwest) had more neighbors to contend and compete with than had younger cities (often in the South and West). (See Boxes 1.5 and 3.5.) Lesser "racial gradients" in the South and West raised fewer social and political barriers to a city's outward expansion. And being the hub of a more rapidly growing metro area created a more expansionist outlook among local public officials than was true of political leadership within more slowly expanding areas.

Finally, the relative unity or fragmentation of local government and institutions influences racial and economic segregation. Table 2.14 summarizes the rough picture in terms of local units of general government. The percentage of the area's population that is governed by the central city is listed in the first column. In effect, this statistic tells what proportion of the metro community falls under a single planning and zoning authority.

What does it mean for a zero-elasticity or low-elasticity city to have planning and zoning authority over about one-quarter of the metro area population? It means little, because that city is no longer planning for new growth that can capture a share of the middle-class, suburban-style population.

TABLE 2.14
LITTLE BOXES REGIONS FOSTER SEGREGATION;
BIG BOX REGIONS FACILITATE INTEGRATION

Type of metro area	Percentage of metro population governed by central city	Metropolitan Power Diffusion Index, 2007	Segregation index,[a] 2010	
			Blacks	Economic
Zero elasticity	21	7.35	63	39
Low elasticity	25	5.51	57	35
Medium elasticity	30	4.26	48	32
High elasticity	37	4.16	51	35
Hyper elasticity	48	3.43	44	34

a. Segregation index: scale 0 to 100 (100 = total apartheid); lower numbers represent improvement.

By contrast, it is significant when a hyper-elasticity city represents almost half the area because that city is planning for and capturing half the area's suburban-style growth. How an elastic city government shapes the mix and distribution of new housing, new shopping areas, and new business parks makes a big difference in the future racial and economic profile of the area.

The second column in Table 2.14 summarizes the results of the Metropolitan Power Diffusion Index, or MPDI (see Box 2.4). Devised by Dr. David Y. Miller of the University of Pittsburgh, the MPDI calculates the degree to which responsibility for 11 public

---

Box 2.4 Little Boxes Split Society and Slow the Economy

The University of Pittsburgh's David Y. Miller has published a short but definitive book, *The Regional Governing of Metropolitan America*.[a] On the basis of rigorous statistical research of all metro areas, Miller reaches key findings about the impact of governmental fragmentation (which Miller labels "diffusion"). He writes:

- "Even when accounting for population [size] and region [of the country], jurisdictional diffusion is significantly and unquestionably linked to Black segregation in metropolitan America."[b]

- "At least historically, power devolved to the local governments within the state creates the necessary condition for greater economic performance. However, when local governments fail to unify that devolved authority at the metropolitan level, the opportunity is lost.... Centralized state systems and decentralized metropolitan region systems underperform, in economic development, empowered but more centralized metropolitan regions."[c]

- "Too much diffusion of power in metropolitan areas serves to increase the probability of racial segregation and to deter the ability of the metropolitan region to take advantage of economic expansion occurring within the region."[d]

- "Gaps between rich and poor communities will always be a part of the metropolitan environment.... However, the distance between rich and poor should be minimized or, at least, kept from widening.... In the Allegheny county case, the gap between the richer and poorer communities is growing—and at an alarming rate.... Indeed, competition feeds upon itself and makes the competitive more competitive and the non-competitive more non-competitive."[e]

services is either centralized or diffused at the local government level. The higher the index number, the more government responsibilities are diffused or decentralized. With one dominant central city (62 percent of the four-county region's population) and one other substantial city (Rio Rancho, population 87,521), but otherwise only 14 other small towns and villages, metro Albuquerque's MPDI was 2.78 in 2007.[18] With 96 suburban governments and a shrinking central city (22 percent of the three-county region's population), metro Syracuse's MPDI was 6.42 in 2007. In parallel with my concept of little boxes and Big Box regions, zero-elasticity regions have the

To quantify the degree of governmental fragmentation, Miller has developed a Metropolitan Power Diffusion Index. The MPDI is a single score that measures how many separate local, county, and special-district governments provide 11 common public services and how much each of those governments spends in providing those services. The services measured include central staff services (including planning and zoning), police, fire, public buildings, roads, housing and community development, libraries, sewerage, solid waste management, water utilities, and financial administration. (A separate MPDI is calculated for public education.) The more individual governments there are that spend greater amounts of money on the services, the higher the MPDI score.

Of the larger regions targeted in Chapter 2, Miller's MPDI rated the 10 most governmentally diffuse regions as Pittsburgh, Chicago, Boston, St. Louis, Minneapolis–St. Paul, Philadelphia, Detroit, Newark, Cincinnati, and Cleveland; the 10 most centralized regions were Anchorage, Reno, Huntsville, Las Vegas, Mobile, San Jose, Fort Wayne, Colorado Springs, Tucson, and Fayetteville.

The MPDI is a powerful analytic tool for investigating why Big Box regions outperform little boxes regions (see Box 2.7, later in this chapter).

a. David Y. Miller, *The Regional Governing of Metropolitan America* (Boulder, CO: Westview Press, 2002).
b. Ibid., 127.
c. Ibid., 130.
d. Ibid.
e. Ibid., 138–43.

greatest diffusion (an MPDI of 7.35 in 2007) and hyper-elasticity regions have the greatest concentration (3.43) of local government responsibility.

The fragmentation of planning and zoning authority among multiple suburban governments in zero-elasticity areas is serious because these suburban governments are planning for most of the area's new growth. Balkanization of the suburbs in these areas inevitably promotes exclusive planning and zoning. By contrast, suburban balkanization around more elastic cities is both less widespread and less significant because these independent suburban governments are typically planning for less than half the area's expansion. In fact, often the central city is guiding suburban growth through extraterritorial planning powers or collaborative arrangements with the county government.

Table 2.15 relates the relative unity or fragmentation of public education to racial segregation in public school systems metro-wide. The same racial and economic patterns characterized elementary school enrollments as occurred in housing markets. With the city schools surrounded by a plethora of suburban little boxes districts, schools in inelastic areas were notably more segregated than schools in more elastic, less fragmented regions. However, in the 1970s and

TABLE 2.15
LITTLE BOXES SCHOOL DISTRICTS FOSTER SEGREGATION;
BIG BOX SCHOOL DISTRICTS FACILITATE INTEGRATION

Type of metro area	Percentage of metro area pupils enrolled in city schools, 1999–2000	Metropolitan Power Diffusion Index for schools, 1992	Elementary school segregation index,[a] 1999–2000	
			Blacks	Economic
Zero elasticity	29	6.12	73	56
Low elasticity	31	4.65	67	50
Medium elasticity	35	3.76	60	46
High elasticity	41	3.12	57	43
Hyper elasticity	45	3.15	51	45

a. Segregation index: scale 0 to 100 (100 = total apartheid); lower numbers represent improvement.

1980s, with large, often county-wide school districts under federal desegregation orders, southern schools were more integrated than southern neighborhoods. During the 1990s and 2000s, however, a more conservative federal judiciary steadily dismantled desegregation plans, sending Black children back to neighborhood schools that were racially and economically segregated. (See Box 2.5 for the impact of economic segregation compared to economic integration on educating low-income children.)

Do these differences in the degree of fragmentation of local government and local education help explain the differences in racial and economic segregation among different metro areas? I believe they do, according to my analysis, the excellent scholarship of others (see Box 2.4), and my personal experience as an elected public official.

It matters whether a mayor or school board member shaping local policy sees poor Blacks, Hispanics, and Asians as "our people here" or "those people over there." Too often suburban officials (and they are still usually White) see "those people over there" when they look at the declining, decaying, impoverished, minority-dominated inner city. Too often city officials (and they are increasingly Black and Hispanic) see only what can be done immediately for "our people here" when confronted with the still overwhelmingly White "outer city."

The unspoken mission of most little boxes town councils and little boxes school boards is "to keep our town (or our schools) just the way they are for people just like *us*" — whoever *us* happens to be. In a more unified area, a Big Box mayor or school board member will often see all groups as common constituents, deserving to be served in a fair and equitable way.

What is the interaction between economic trends and these patterns of metro development? The relationship between a central city's economic health and its suburbs' economic health has provoked lively debate in recent years. Many suburbanites believe they are economically independent of the city. Certainly many examples of highly prosperous individual suburban communities exist outside the most depressed central cities, such as Bloomfield Hills outside Detroit. And with the increasing migration of jobs to suburban office complexes and industrial parks, many argue that "edge cities" are the wave of the future and or even that, in the Internet Age, cities will become superfluous.

The bulk of evidence, however, supports the view that cities and suburbs are all in it together. All are part of a regional economy

Box 2.5 Housing Policy Is School Policy

In 1966, sociologist James Coleman released his pathbreaking study, *Equality of Educational Opportunity*.[a] Sponsored by the then U.S. Office of Education, the Coleman report concluded that the socioeconomic characteristics of a child and of the child's classmates (measured principally by family income and parental education) were the overwhelming factors that accounted for academic success. Nothing else—expenditures per pupil, pupil–teacher ratios, teacher experience, instructional materials, age of school buildings, and so on—came close.

"The educational resources provided by a child's fellow students," Coleman summarized, "are more important for his achievement than are the resources provided by the school board." So important are fellow students, the report found, that "the social composition of the student body is more highly related to achievement, independent of the student's own social background, than is any school factor."[b]

In the almost five decades since, no finding of education researchers (including almost two dozen of my own studies) has been more consistent—and no research finding has been more consistently ignored by most politicians and many educators. They will not challenge the underlying racial and class structure of American society.

The definitive research into the impact of economically integrated classrooms on low-income children's academic achievement levels has now been carried out by Dr. Heather Schwartz.[c] She analyzed up to seven years of test scores for 858 children from public housing families in Montgomery County, Maryland. With the nation's oldest and largest inclusionary zoning program (see Box 3.1) and a highly rated county-wide school district, Montgomery County provided the perfect laboratory for testing the effectiveness of economic school integration. Public housing children do not live in projects but in housing authority–owned townhouses and private apartment complexes scattered throughout the country's 11th-highest-income county.

whose overall fortunes are shaped primarily by constant changes in technology, consumer tastes, competition (increasingly global), transportation and communications links, investment capital flows, labor force quality, and other economic forces. One very compelling new theory of economic development is that America has entered an age where much economic development is driven by where

Schwartz's findings are summarized in two charts. The "Red Zone" school lines show how well public housing children closed the gaps in higher-poverty schools that were receiving substantial extra resources from the school district (such as full-day kindergarten, smaller class sizes, intensive teacher training, and a 20 percent boost in per pupil expenditures). After modest gains in the early grades, the public housing children fell further behind district averages as they approached their teens.

Public housing children in the low-poverty "Green Zone" schools received no special assistance. They merely benefited from being surrounded by classmates from much higher-income, more highly educated families. As they approached their teenage years, their test scores soared, and they rapidly closed the gaps.

Schwartz found that two-thirds of the children's success was attributable to attending high socioeconomic status schools and one-third to living in high socioeconomic status neighborhoods. In other words, where a child lives largely shapes the child's educational opportunities—not in terms of how much money is being spent per pupil but in terms of who the child's classmates are. Housing policy is school policy.

a. James Coleman, *Equality of Educational Opportunity* (Washington, D.C.: U.S. Office of Education, 1966).

b. Quoted in Richard D. Kahlenberg, *All Together Now: Creating Middle-Class Schools through Public School Choice* (Washington, DC: Brookings Institution Press, 2001), 28. Kahlenberg's 33 pages of footnotes to Chapters 3 and 4 catalog most major studies on the effects of racial and economic school integration.

c. See Heather Schwartz, "Housing Policy Is School Policy: Economically Integrative Housing Promotes Academic Success in Montgomery County, Maryland," The Century Foundation, New York, 2010, http://tcf.org/publications/pdfs/housing-policy-is-school-policy-pdf/Schwartz.pdf. The report is based on Schwartz's doctoral dissertation for Columbia University.

members of the "creative class" cluster (see Box 2.6). People do not move to jobs; jobs move to where talented, highly creative people choose to live, largely for quality-of-life considerations.

One dramatic economic trend in recent decades has been the deindustrialization of the American economy. In 1950, for example, the largest segment of the American workforce (30 percent) was en-

Box 2.6 The Rise of the Creative Class

"Why Cities without Gays and Rock Bands Are Losing the Economic Development Race": the subtitle of the May 2002 *Washington Monthly* article summarizing Richard Florida's just-published book, *The Rise of the Creative Class*, was certainly eye catching.[a] And his explanation was thought provoking.

"Talented people seek an environment open to differences," Florida wrote. "Many highly creative people, regardless of ethnic background or sexual orientation, grew up feeling like outsiders, different in some way from their classmates. When they are sizing up a new company and community, acceptance of diversity and of gays in particular is a sign that reads 'non-standard people welcome here.'"

And rock bands? "The [creative people] I talked to also desired nightlife with a wide mix of options. The most highly valued options were experiential ones—interesting music venues, neighborhood art galleries, performance spaces, and theaters. A vibrant, varied nightlife was viewed by many as another signal that a city 'gets it,' even by those who infrequently partake in nightlife. More than anything, the creative class craves real experiences in the real world."

"The creative class," Florida argued, "[is] a fast growing, highly educated, and well-paid segment of the workforce on whose efforts corporate profits and economic growth increasingly depend. Members of the creative class do a wide variety of work in a wide variety of industries—from technology to entertainment, journalism to finance, high-end manufacturing to the arts.... Places that succeed in attracting creative class people prosper; those that don't fail."

Florida developed a "Creativity Index" with a mix of four equally weighted factors that ranks all metro areas: creative class share of the workforce; percentage of high-tech industry; innovation, as measured by patents per capita; and diversity, as measured by the Gay Index (see http://www.creativeclass.org).

gaged in manufacturing; by 2009, the proportion of manufacturing workers had dropped to just 7 percent (and many of these workers were not production employees but designers, engineers, marketing executives, and accountants working for manufacturing companies).

Trends in manufacturing jobs (Table 2.16) reveal that deindustrialization hit inelastic areas hard. Though manufacturing's share of employment has dropped steadily since 1950, the number of in-

Among giant metro areas (1 million or more residents), the top ranked is (not surprisingly) the San Francisco Bay Area, followed by Austin, San Diego, Boston, and Seattle. The bottom 5 (of 49) are Louisville, Buffalo, Las Vegas, Norfolk–Virginia Beach–Newport News, and Memphis.

For large metro areas (500,000 to 1 million), Albuquerque is top ranked, while Youngstown–Warren ranks last. Among medium-sized metro areas (250,000 to 500,000), Madison is number one; Shreveport brings up the rear. Santa Fe (with both a vigorous cultural scene and Los Alamos National Laboratory) heads the list of small metro areas (50,000 to 250,000), while Enid, Oklahoma, ranks last in the Creativity Index rankings.

"While it is important to have a solid business climate," Florida counseled, "having an effective people climate is even more essential. By this I mean a general strategy aimed at attracting and retaining people—especially, but not limited to, creative people. This entails remaining open to diversity and actively working to cultivate it, and investing in the lifestyle amenities that people really want and use often [urban parks, bike lanes, performance venues], as opposed to using financial incentives to attract companies, build professional sports stadiums, or develop retail complexes."

a. Richard Florida, *The Rise of the Creative Class and How It's Transforming Work, Leisure, Community and Everyday Life* (New York: Basic Books, 2002); Richard Florida, "The Rise of the Creative Class: Why Cities without Gays and Rock Bands Are Losing the Economic Development Race," *Washington Monthly*, May 2002. All quotes are from the *Washington Monthly* article. Also, see Florida's *Who's Your City? How the Creative Economy Is Making Where to Live the Most Important Decision of Your Life* (New York: Basic Books, 2008).

dustrial jobs grew in almost all metro areas until the early 1970s. Between 1969 and 2000, 31 zero-elasticity regions lost 2.8 million manufacturing jobs (a devastating drop of 42 percent). The 27 low-elasticity regions lost another million manufacturing jobs (a drop of 24 percent), but manufacturing jobs increased in medium-, high-, and hyper-elasticity metro areas. For all 137 metro areas, manufacturing employment slid downward from 14.4 million to 13.3 mil-

TABLE 2.16
INELASTIC REGIONS WERE HARDER HIT BY DEINDUSTRIALIZATION OF AMERICAN LABOR MARKET

Type of metro area	Manufacturing jobs as percentage of total jobs		Percentage change in manufacturing jobs		Manufacturing jobs (NAICS) as percentage of total jobs, 2009	Percentage change in manufacturing jobs (SIC and NAICS), 1969–2009
	Census, 1950	SIC, 1969	SIC, 1969–2000	NAICS, 2001–09		
Zero elasticity	33	25	−42	−32	6	−67
Low elasticity	32	26	−24	−29	8	−52
Medium elasticity	21	18	+29	−12	6	−10
High elasticity	22	20	+24	−20	7	−7
Hyper elasticity	14	16	+77	−27	6	+17

Note: SIC = Standard Industrial Classification; NAICS = North American Industry Classification System.

lion jobs (a loss of about 8 percent) between 1969 and 2000. These decades best illustrate long-term trends.

During the 2000s (an initial recession, followed by a largely jobless recovery, followed by the Great Recession), factory jobs took a double-digit beating almost everywhere. By 2009, the proportion of manufacturing employment in all these target regions basically clustered around the national metropolitan average of 7 percent. Undoubtedly, the slow recovery under way will restore some manufacturing employment, but factory jobs will never play the pivotal economic role that they did a half-century ago.

Clearly, there is a regional pattern here. Is the deindustrialization of one part of the country and the modest industrialization of another part a simple Frost Belt–Sun Belt phenomenon? In part, yes. Most of the old, smokestack industries that were driven out of business by international competition were located in the Northeast or the industrial Midwest. Jobs in certain industries (for example, steel and aluminum), once lost, are rarely re-created elsewhere in the country. Other industrial jobs relocated from the Frost Belt to the Sun Belt.

In large part, however, the growth in manufacturing in the South and West was not based on export products but on goods that serve primarily growing local markets (for example, bakeries, dairy products, or printing). And even when the number of factory jobs grew, the relative importance of manufacturing in the local economy declined in almost all metro areas.[19]

Urban areas, however, are not simply passive beneficiaries or victims of economic changes. Local areas can shape their futures. Detroit, for example, may have lost massive numbers of auto industry jobs, but other areas of the country have added automotive jobs (for example, Arlington, Texas, in the Dallas–Ft. Worth area; Smyrna, Tennessee, in the Nashville–Murfreesboro area; or Greenville–Spartanburg, South Carolina). An aging plant may be closed as obsolete, but its home region need not lose its replacement. Moreover, an area can certainly nurture or compete for new businesses that offer new types of products and new types of services, which are the basis of most new export jobs.

Each region has attractions in terms of the lifestyle it can offer. The Sun Belt does not have an inherent advantage over the Frost Belt. Many older cities, for example, have cultural facilities and institutions that are superior to those in newer cities. Climate and geography are matters of taste and adjustment. Inelastic areas are not without intrinsic competitive advantages.

Where many inelastic areas have declined is in the ability to compete. Business seeks out labor markets and economic regions, rarely specific government jurisdictions. But economic development is a private–public partnership, and the capabilities of the public partner are vital. Typically, a strong, healthy, elastic central city is a metropolitan area's dominant and most capable public partner. This type of city has broad planning and zoning powers (often with extraterritorial planning jurisdiction) and often directly owns major infrastructure systems (e.g., water supply and sewage treatment). With its broad tax base, an elastic city can finance the public infrastructure needed to support major private investment. And it has the power to make major decisions. As Harvey Gantt, former mayor of hyper-elastic Charlotte, observed, metro areas "with fewer governmental entities have a definite advantage in quicker decision making, building regional consensus, and moving forward on large initiatives."[20]

By contrast, who speaks and acts for greater Detroit or greater Cleveland, which suffer from high political fragmentation, strong

---

Box 2.7 Economic Competitiveness Hurt by Metro Fragmentation

Professor Jerry R. Paytas (Carnegie Mellon University) systematically applied the Metropolitan Power Diffusion Index to a multidecade analysis of economic development among all metro areas. Paytas found that "Controlling for national trends and industrial composition, metropolitan competitiveness is adversely affected by metropolitan fragmentation…. The impact on the smallest metropolitan areas is most severe…. Smaller areas with fragmented metropolitan governance may lack the scope and power to affect the challenges they face. The large negative impact of fragmentation indicates that unity could help resolve the kinds of cross-jurisdictional challenges that are needed for a region to be competitive. These challenges include transportation and infrastructure as well as workforce and social issues."[a]

Paytas further observed that "Long-term competitiveness requires flexibility, and fragmented regions are less likely to mobilize the consensus for change…. Fragmented regions divide the regional constituency, offering opponents of change more opportunities, forums, and even institutional support to resist change…. Unification encourages serving the regional constituency rather than parochial interests."[b]

racial divisions, sharp income differentials, and interjurisdictional competition—in short, from the loss of a shared sense of community and common destiny metro-wide (see Box 2.7)?

Table 2.17 summarizes the rates of job creation in nonmanufacturing occupations. As with comparing rates of population growth, allowances must be made for the different bases on which growth rates are calculated. Nevertheless, more elastic regions (generally, in the South and West) have outperformed less elastic regions (generally, in the Northeast and Midwest) by substantial margins. Even with the flowering of the Information Age economy, more elastic areas had double the rates of nonmanufacturing job creation than did less elastic areas. This raises the old chicken or egg dilemma: which came first—new jobs or new people?

An even more complex picture is presented in Table 2.18, which shows the rate of growth in inflation-adjusted (or "real") median family income metro-wide over a 60-year period (1950–2009). The analyses presented to this point would suggest that growth in real incomes should be least in zero-elasticity areas and scale steadily

---

Why would this be the case? Among explanations offered by Paytas and others are

- Cutthroat intermunicipal competition over industrial and commercial prospects
- Uncontrolled peripheral sprawl and core community abandonment
- High cost of new infrastructure in peripheral communities
- Waste of existing infrastructure in core communities
- Unnecessary duplication of services

To this list, I would add an inability to access and develop the region's full resources. One casualty is the wasted talents of students trapped in high-poverty school districts in little boxes regions (see Box 2.5). Another would be the inability to tap a region's full tax base for major infrastructure initiatives to promote economic development (see Table 2.20, later in this chapter).

a. Jerry Paytas, "Does Governance Matter? The Dynamics of Metropolitan Governance and Competitiveness," Carnegie Mellon Center for Economic Development, Pittsburgh, PA, December 2001, 15, 20.
b. Ibid., 22–23.

Table 2.17
Elastic Areas Had Faster Rates of Nonfactory Job Creation
Than Did Inelastic Areas

Type of metro area	Percentage change in nonmanufacturing jobs		
	SIC, 1969–2000	NAICS, 2001–09	SIC and NAICS, 1969–2009
Zero elasticity	69	6	82
Low elasticity	98	5	110
Medium elasticity	184	9	219
High elasticity	163	11	196
Hyper elasticity	215	16	270

Note: SIC = Standard Industrial Classification; NAICS = North American Industry Classification System.

Table 2.18
Elastic Areas Showed Greater Real Income Gains
Than Did Inelastic Areas

Type of area	Inflation-adjusted growth in metro median family income, 1950–2009	Inflation-adjusted growth in city median family income, 1950–2009
Zero elasticity	128	46
Low elasticity	104	56
Medium elasticity	119	80
High elasticity	127	90
Hyper elasticity	136	110

upward to the highest rates in hyper-elasticity areas. Instead, with 128 percent growth in real median family income, the zero-elasticity group outperformed the low-elasticity group (104 percent) and the medium-elasticity group (119 percent) and, in effect, tied with high-elasticity regions (127 percent). Zero-elasticity regions did lag slightly the hyper-elasticity regions (136 percent).

Closer examination shows that average real income growth for the zero-elasticity group was buoyed by the powerful economic performances of America's flagship postindustrial regions, in the corridor from Boston to Washington, D.C. Traditional downtowns prospered as national and international centers of financial, information, government, and business services. Close-in historic neighborhoods were revived by thousands of young professionals and empty nesters moving in, seeking the cultural vitality of city life (and no commuting to their high-tech jobs in the city's office towers, universities, and medical complexes). Around the outlying beltways, other Information Age businesses blossomed. As metropolitan regions, New York, Boston, San Francisco, Washington, D.C., and their brethren maintained their national economic leadership.

However, such regions are less prosperous than they might appear statistically. In its reports, the Census Bureau treats a dollar as having the same buying power everywhere. In reality, great differences exist in relative costs of living among different metropolitan areas.[21] Table 2.19 adjusts median family income in 2009 for differences in cost of living. Adjusted for an average cost-of-living index of 118, the average median family income of $74,217 for zero-elasticity *regions* becomes $62,947 in terms of real standard of living. In effect, after cost-of-living adjustments, all five elasticity categories have roughly the same real median family income.

However, adjusted for cost of living, the disparity in median family income among elasticity categories for *central cities* already apparent in nominal dollars becomes even more pronounced in cost-of-living-adjusted dollars. Compared to the zero-elasticity cities' median family income of $38,571, medium-, high-, and hyper-elasticity cities' median family incomes are 42 percent, 40 percent, and 56 percent higher.

From city hall's perspective, municipal bond ratings remain a key indicator of a city's long-term economic health (Table 2.20). Although zero-elasticity cities are in the wealthiest metro areas (at least, nominally), they have bond ratings that are lower than those of their municipal counterparts in other categories. By early 2012, the average bond rating of zero-elasticity cities (A2–) was *four* steps below the average rating of hyper-elasticity cities (Aa1–). Only Minneapolis and Seattle of the 58 inelastic cities had Aaa bond ratings, while 15 of the 79 elastic cities were rated blue-chip investments.[22]

The Point of (Almost) No Return

In the first editions of *Cities without Suburbs*, I observed that 24 cities had experienced major population loss (a change of –20 percent or

TABLE 2.19

COST-OF-LIVING ADJUSTMENTS EQUALIZE METRO MEDIAN FAMILY INCOMES BUT SHOW MUCH HIGHER INCOMES WITHIN ELASTIC CITIES

Type of area	Metro median family income, 2005–09 ($)	City median family income, 2005–09 ($)	Urban COL, 2008 ($)	COL-adjusted metro median family income, 2005–09 ($)	COL-adjusted city median family income, 2005–09 ($)
Zero elasticity (24 areas)	74,217	45,476	118	62,947	38,571
Low elasticity (19 areas)	67,745	53,014	107	63,245	49,492
Medium elasticity (19 areas)	62,085	53,931	99	63,028	54,750
High elasticity (23 areas)	60,435	53,203	98	61,394	54,047
Hyper elasticity (23 areas)	63,806	59,805	99	64,202	60,176

Note: COL = cost of living. Table covers metro areas for which COL indices were available.

TABLE 2.20
ELASTIC CITIES HAVE BETTER BOND RATINGS THAN DO INELASTIC CITIES

Central city	City bond rating score	City bond rating (average)
Zero elasticity	5.8	A2–
Low elasticity	7.2	Aa3–
Medium elasticity	7.8	Aa2–
High elasticity	8.1	Aa2+
Hyper elasticity	8.3	Aa1–

Source: Moody's Investor Services.
Note: Aaa = 10.0; Aa1 = 8.5; Aa2 = 8.0; Aa3 = 7.5; A1 = 6.5; A2 = 6.0;
A3 = 5.5; aa1 = 4.5; Baa2 = 4.0; Baa3 = 3.5; Ba1 = 2.5; Ba2 = 2.0; Ba3 = 1.5.

more) and had a disproportionate minority population (typically, three, four, five, or more times the percentage of minorities in the suburbs). Moreover, and most important, their residents had average income levels that were less than 70 percent of suburban income levels. These 24 cities seemed to have passed a point of no return. I called it a point of no return because, throughout the 1970s and 1980s, despite redevelopment projects, enterprise zones, and neighborhood empowerment programs, *no city past the point of no return ever closed the economic gap with its suburbs by as much as a single percentage point!*

In addition, another 13 cities passed all three milestones during the 1990s and joined the list of cities past the point of no return (Table 2.21).

As a result of the economic boom of the mid- to late-1990s, however, I renamed the list "Cities Past the Point of (Almost) No Return." During the 1990s, 10 of the original 24 cities did close the income gap with their suburbs. In the past decade, though, 9 of these 10 resumed their longer-term downward trend. Only Chicago continued to close the income gap during the 2000s.

Chicago can justly lay claim to being a comeback city. Chicago's resurging average income rose from 69.2 percent of suburban levels in 1989 to 74.7 percent in 1999 to 84.6 percent in 2009. The income gap was closed because of construction of thousands of new, middle-class townhouses around the Loop; conversion of several massive public housing projects into mixed-income communities;

TABLE 2.21
WHAT HAPPENED TO THE ORIGINAL 37 CITIES PAST THE POINT OF (ALMOST) NO RETURN IN 2000s?

City (peak year if not 1950)	State	Percentage change in households, 1950–2010 or peak year to 2010	Percentage change in population, 1950–2010 or peak year to 2010	Black and Hispanic percentage of city population, 2010	Black and Hispanic percentage of suburban population, 2010	City:suburb ratio of Black and Hispanic population, 2010 (suburb = 1)	City income as percentage of suburban income		
							1989	1999	2009
CHICAGO[a]	IL	-4	-26	61.3	28.4	2.2	69.2	74.7	84.6

Escaped point of (almost) no return

Income gap still widening

City (peak year if not 1950)	State	Percentage change in households	Percentage change in population	Black and Hispanic % of city pop., 2010	Black and Hispanic % of suburban pop., 2010	City:suburb ratio	1989	1999	2009
BENTON HARBOR[a] (1960)	MI	-42	-48	86.5	13.5	6.4	42.5	45.2	38.1
East St. Louis[a]	IL	-58	-67	98.2	15.9	6.2	41.4	47.5	40.3
NEWARK[a]	NJ	-22	-37	83.6	28.5	2.9	38.3	38.1	40.4
HARTFORD[a]	CT	-12	-30	78.9	13.8	5.7	53.4	46.6	40.6
TRENTON[a]	NJ	-11	-34	83.5	19.8	4.2	50.3	45.4	41.8
READING[b]	PA	-7	-19	68.1	7.4	9.2	70.4	55.7	42.5
CAMDEN[a]	NJ	-29	-38	91.4	20.4	4.5	42.6	39.5	43.0
YORK[b]	PA	-12	-31	48.6	4.8	10.1	71.4	61.1	48.1
East Chicago[a] (1960)	IN	-36	-49	91.7	16.6	5.5	61.1	58.4	49.7
DETROIT[a]	MI	-47	-61	89.0	13.2	6.7	52.6	53.6	50.7
CLEVELAND[a]	OH	-37	-57	62.4	14.3	4.4	54.5	55.9	54.4
GARY[a] (1960)	IN	-38	-55	89.0	16.6	5.4	60.5	62.1	54.7
Pontiac[b] (1970)	MI	-13	-30	67.6	13.2	5.1	54.9	57.7	56.9
FLINT[a] (1960)	MI	-31	-48	60.0	12.0	5.0	68.9	68.6	58.4
ROCHESTER[b]	NY	-18	-40	55.9	7.5	7.5	71.1	66.4	58.8
SAGINAW[a] (1960)	MI	-31	-48	54.2	14.1	3.8	63.8	63.4	59.1
DAYTON[a] (1960)	OH	-27	-46	45.6	11.1	4.1	64.4	66.7	60.2

YOUNGSTOWN[a] (1930)	OH	-31	-61	53.2	5.7	9.3	66.1	66.5	60.3
HARRISBURG[b]	PA	-25	-45	68.0	9.2	7.4	71.2	68.2	60.8
BALTIMORE[a]	MD	-7	-35	67.5	22.3	3.0	64.3	63.0	62.2
ELMIRA[b]	NY	-25	-41	14.9	4.1	3.6	70.4	69.7	64.5
AKRON[b] (1960)	OH	-7	-31	33.3	5.6	5.9	76.1	71.9	64.8
PROVIDENCE[b] (1940)	RI	-7	-30	51.2	8.8	5.8	75.9	67.1	65.3
Holyoke[a] (1920)	MA	-6	-34	50.8	7.4	6.9	72.8	72.3	66.7
SYRACUSE[b]	NY	-10	-34	36.3	4.0	9.1	76.9	69.8	66.8
BUFFALO[a]	NY	-32	-55	47.9	5.3	9.0	70.5	67.3	69.7
26-city average		-24	-42	64.5	12.1	5.3	61.8	59.5	54.6
Still wide income gap but net gain in households									
BRIDGEPORT[a]	CT	11	-9	70.4	12.1	43.7	35.7	35.7	35.8
North Chicago[a] (1970)	IL	6	-31	61.9	15.0	43.3	58.5	58.5	53.7
PHILADELPHIA[a]	PA	3	-26	54.5	13.6	61.7	57.4	57.4	55.9
NEW HAVEN[a]	CT	4	-21	60.8	22.1	64.5	60.0	60.0	61.8
New Bedford[b] (1920)	MA	16	-22	21.9	8.8	70.0	67.4	67.4	63.0
Fall River[b] (1920)	MA	20	-26	10.8	8.8	70.3	69.7	69.7	65.3
6-city average		10	-23	46.7	13.4	58.9	58.1	58.1	55.9
Narrowed income gap but lost households									
CANTON[b]	OH	-15	-38	26.6	4.6	74.6	73.0	73.0	70.4
BIRMINGHAM[a] (1960)	AL	-12	-38	76.8	22.1	69.2	67.7	67.7	71.0
ATLANTIC CITY[a] (1940)	NJ	-13	-38	62.7	24.5	71.4	69.7	69.7	72.1
ST. LOUIS[a]	MO	-45	-63	52.5	15.9	69.6	68.6	68.6	75.0
4-city average		-21	-44	54.7	16.8	71.2	69.8	69.8	72.1

Note: Italics indicate not designated as central city per 1990 census; CAPITAL LETTERS indicate the principal city in the metro area.
a. Designated as central city per 1990 census.
b. Designated as central city per 2000 census.

effective work by neighborhood revitalization groups; and most important, an economic boom that, toward the late 1990s, finally cut unemployment and raised incomes in many inner-city neighborhoods—a trend that was reversed when the Great Recession hit in 2008 but was not yet fully reflected in the 2009 income data.

However, the city–suburban income gap also closed because of the steady suburbanization of poverty that was occurring, particularly in Chicago's south suburbs. In fact, Chicago illustrates the twin trends that allowed several cities to begin reversing the city–suburban income gap: gentrification of central city neighborhoods and corresponding falling incomes and rising poverty levels in inner suburbs.

For this edition, I have rethought the criterion of major population loss (a change of −20 percent or more since a city's peak population). Implicitly, I had believed that at about a 20 percent level of raw population loss, a city begins to lose households. However, for this edition, I have tracked down household counts for most cities from the 1950 census or earlier (difficult to locate), compared them to household counts from Census 2010 (readily available), and found that some inelastic cities that otherwise show significant population losses have also experienced net gains in number of households (review Box 1.7).

Number of households equals number of occupied housing units and translates into number of residential property taxpayers. From city hall's perspective, the key issue is not numbers of residents but numbers of taxpayers. Moreover, a big difference exists between a city whose population loss results in abandoned, boarded-up houses and weed-overgrown vacant lots and a city whose population loss reflects smaller households and new townhouses and apartments being built for them.

Thus, Table 2.21 divides the 37 declining cities into four groups:

- Chicago, which escaped the point of (almost) no return
- Twenty-six cities still meeting all three criteria, as a group averaging a 24 percent loss of households, a minority population over five times suburban levels, and a steadily widening city–suburban income gap (from 61.8 percent in 1989 to 59.5 percent in 1999 to 54.6 percent in 2009)
- Six cities, including Philadelphia, that still have a wide city–suburban income gap (averaging 55.9 percent) and a disproportionate minority population (three and one-half times suburban levels), but actually added households (10 percent) despite a 23 percent loss of population since their population peaks (which occurred in 1950 in 21 of 37 cases in Table 2.21)

- Four cities, including St. Louis, that have lost households (a change of –21 percent) and have disproportionate minority populations (over three times suburban levels) but whose city–suburb income gap had risen above the "magic" 70 percent level I have applied

In addition, 10 more cities passed all three milestones during the 2000s and joined the list of cities past the point of (almost) no return (Table 2.22). By 2010, 7 other cities had average incomes that had dropped far below 70 percent of suburban levels and disproportionate concentrations of minority residents but still had experienced household growth. Another 12 cities still had income levels above 70 percent of suburban levels (but trending downward) and had been losing households. Both groups should be considered on a "watch list" in coming years.

Between the two lists, 13 cities had lost their designation as central cities in recent decades.[23] As profligate as the federal government became after Census 2000 in designating "principal cities" (née central cities), particularly in major metro areas in the Sun Belt (review Box 2.2), these 13 cities' loss of designation is as telling a measure of their decline as my statistics.

These cities in Tables 2.21 and 2.22 share a common personality: all of the cities (except Birmingham) are zero- and low-elasticity cities and all (except Baltimore and Birmingham) are located in little boxes regions.

Even when better economic times return, the continued division of urban America by race and class will throw a dark shadow over the futures of many of these cities.

Cities without Suburbs

The cities in Tables 2.21 and 2.22 are doing very poorly even though many are located in some of the country's nominally wealthiest metro areas. This section examines the other extreme—cities that are doing well even though they are often located in more modest-income metro areas. These are all cities that dominate their areas. They are, in effect, cities without suburbs (Table 2.23).

I have applied three standards to identify a city without suburbs. First, the city must house at least 70 percent or more of the urbanized population. On that basis, for example, prominent cities such as Oklahoma City and Nashville miss the cut. Second, the average

TABLE 2.22
NEW CITIES PAST THE POINT OF (ALMOST) NO RETURN BY 2010

City (peak year if not 1950)	State	Percentage change in households, 1950–2010	Percentage change in population, 1950 or peak year to 2010	Black and Hispanic percentage of city population, 2010	Black and Hispanic percentage of suburban population, 2010	City:suburb ratio of Black and Hispanic population, 2010 (suburb = 1)	City income as percentage of suburban income		
							1989	1999	2009
10 new cities past the point of (almost) no return									
Chicago Heights (1970)	IL	-19	-26	74.7	28.4	2.6	67.8	53.1	51.4
Newburgh	NY	-10	-10	73.8	16.5	4.5	60.1	57.0	51.6
MILWAUKEE (1960)	WI	-0.3	-20	56.5	7.0	8.1	62.2	57.6	54.9
LIMA (1970)	OH	-19	-28	26.0	5.7	4.6	73.2	70.8	55.2
McKeesport (1940)	PA	-42	-64	33.7	6.8	5.0	65.0	62.8	57.2
Easton	PA	-9	-25	35.3	8.0	4.4	71.4	67.4	61.2
MUSKEGON	MI	-7	-21	39.1	11.5	3.4	73.0	74.8	64.7
Wilkes–Barre (1940)	PA	-17	-52	21.4	4.1	5.2	83.9	78.5	65.4
ERIE (1960)	PA	-1	-27	32.1	3.1	10.4	80.2	76.1	68.1
Hammond (1960)	IN	-9	-28	55.8	16.6	3.4	77.8	70.2	69.0
10-city average		-13	-30	44.8	10.8	4.2	71.5	66.8	59.9
7 cities on watch list: Growing income gap but household growth									
Paterson	NJ	5	5	86.0	24.4	3.5	46.6	45.3	41.2
Elizabeth	NJ	31	11	78.0	28.5	2.7	49.2	44.2	46.5
New Britain (1970)	CT	2	-12	47.7	13.8	3.5	70.9	63.8	51.3
Allentown	PA	41	11	32.4	8.0	4.1	80.8	68.9	55.9
Norristown	PA	32	-10	63.0	13.6	4.6	69.0	62.5	56.6
Springfield	MA	21	-6	58.4	7.4	7.9	76.1	69.2	59.7

Lorain (1970)	OH	11	-18	41.2	14.3	2.9	62.8	64.0	63.5
7-city average		23	-4	53.5	14.3	3.7	68.1	62.1	55.6
12 cities on watch list: Loss of households but income gaps still above 70 percent									
JACKSON	MI	-17	-34	22.8	7.1	3.2	78.4	70.4	71.0
Schenectady	NY	-6	-31	29.0	4.8	6.0	77.1	70.2	71.5
BAY CITY	MI	-6	-33	10.3	3.4	3.0	79.5	77.8	72.0
Niagara Falls (1960)	NY	-27	-51	24.2	5.3	4.6	73.6	70.6	72.3
UTICA (1930)	NY	-35	-39	21.0	3.2	6.6	86.4	81.4	73.0
Alliance (1960)	OH	-1	-21	12.2	4.6	2.7	72.5	71.3	73.5
Troy	NY	0	-31	23.1	4.8	4.8	71.8	69.1	74.7
POUGHKEEPSIE	NY	-0.2	-20	51.2	16.5	3.1	89.9	71.5	75.0
WILLIAMSPORT	PA	-15	-35	15.8	1.6	9.9	83.9	81.3	76.0
ALTOONA (1930)	PA	-15	-40	4.5	1.5	3.0	88.2	86.0	76.0
JOHNSTOWN (1920)	PA	-26	-69	13.6	2.8	4.9	79.4	82.5	77.0
Sharon (1960)	PA	-22	-47	16.0	5.7	2.8	81.8	79.6	78.8
12-city average		-14	-38	20.3	5.1	4.1	80.2	76.0	74.2

Note: *Italics* indicate not designated as central city for Census 2010; CAPITAL LETTERS indicate the principal city in metro area; lowercase indicates a secondary city.

Table 2.23
44 Cities without Suburbs and Almost Cities without Suburbs

Category	Percentage of urbanized area residents living in city, 2010	City income as percentage of suburban per capita income, 2009	City per capita income, 2005–09 (unadjusted $)	City per capita income, 2005–09 (COL adjusted $)	COL index, 2010	Black and Hispanic percentage of city population, 2010	Black and Hispanic percentage of suburban population, 2010	City:suburb ratio of Black and Hispanic population, 2010 (suburb = 1)	Metro residential segregation index for Blacks, 2010	Moody's bond rating (latest)
				Cities without suburbs						
Anchorage (city and borough), AK	100	133	33,436	26,038	128.4	12.8	4.6	2.8	41	Aa2
Montgomery, AL	78	110	24,972	25,167	99.2	60.3	27.5	2.2	54	Aa2
Lexington–Fayette, KY	98	111	27,878	30,025	92.8	21.2	8.0	2.7	46	Aa2
Corpus Christi, TX	95	108	22,318	24,587	90.8	63.6	54.1	1.2	43	Aa2
Greensboro, NC	86	106	25,493	n.a.	n.a.	47.7	23.9	2.0	54	Aaa
Colorado Springs, CO	74	103	28,114	30,288	92.8	21.9	17.3	1.3	37	Aa3
Fresno, CA	76	95	19,835	16,906	117.3	54.6	55.8	1.0	49	A2
Albuquerque, NM	74	105	25,542	26,414	96.7	50.0	47.2	1.1	29	Aa1
Tallahassee, FL	76	92	22,877	n.a.	n.a.	40.7	35.2	1.2	44	A1
9-city average	**84**	**107**	**26,014**	**25,632**	**102.6**	**41.4**	**30.4**	**1.4**	**44**	**Aa2**
			Almost-cities without suburbs (disproportionate minority ratio)							
Fort Wayne, IN	81	90	23,074	24,441	94.4	23.1	4.1	5.6	58	Aa3
Beaumont, TX	80	98	22,698	23,724	95.7	60.3	16.5	3.7	67	Aa2
Wichita, KS	81	96	24,764	26,962	91.8	26.4	7.4	3.6	55	Aa1
3-city average	**81**	**95**	**23,512**	**25,042**	**94.0**	**36.6**	**9.3**	**3.9**	**60**	**Aa2**
		Almost-cities without suburbs (less than 90 percent of suburban income)								
San Antonio, TX	75	82	21,418	22,389	95.7	69.5	44.9	1.5	48	Aaa

City										
Jacksonville–Duval, FL	77	82	25,223		92.9	37.8	13.1	2.9	52	Aa2
Stockton, CA	79	81	20,090		n.a.	51.8	41.6	1.2	45	Baa1
3-city average	**77**	**82**	**23,321**		**94.3**	**53.0**	**33.2**	**1.6**	**48**	**Aa2**

29 Almost-cities without suburbs (less than 70 percent of urbanized population)

City										
Oklahoma City, OK	67	96	24,445	26,651	91.7	32.0	12.5	2.6	49	Aaa
Shreveport, LA	67	91	21,859	22,937	95.3	57.0	27.4	2.1	56	A1
Durham, NC	66	90	26,822	27,777	96.6	54.6	24.3	2.2	47	Aaa
Bakersfield, CA	66	125	22,601	21,853	103.4	53.2	55.6	1.0	50	A2
Salem, OR	65	97	21,966	n.a.	n.a.	21.6	23.5	0.9	28	A1
Fayetteville, NC	65	111	22,100	23,216	95.2	50.9	38.2	1.3	31	Aa2
Eugene, OR	63	97	23,710	21,586	109.8	9.1	7.7	1.2	23	Aa1
Huntsville, AL	63	106	29,132	31,930	91.2	36.7	18.4	2.0	49	Aaa
Nashville–Davidson, TN	62	105	26,431	29,720	88.9	38.2	11.7	3.3	55	Aa1
Louisville–Jefferson County, KY	61	91	24,436	27,868	87.7	27.1	9.1	3.0	56	Aa2
Memphis, TN	61	80	21,293	24,131	88.2	69.6	32.0	2.2	62	Aa2
Mobile, AL	60	108	22,141	23,882	92.7	52.7	22.7	2.3	59	A1
Tulsa, Okla.	60	106	25,641	28,990	88.4	29.7	7.3	4.1	54	Aa1
Charlotte, NC	59	119	31,839	34,158	93.2	47.5	23.3	2.0	53	Aaa
Boise City, ID	59	121	27,621	28,404	97.2	8.5	15.9	0.5	35	Aa2
Killeen, TX	59	90	19,764	n.a.	n.a.	55.2	31.4	1.8	41	Aa3
Winston-Salem, NC	59	96	24,503	26,508	92.4	48.7	13.1	3.7	56	Aaa
Madison, WI	58	89	28,840	n.a.	n.a.	13.9	7.1	2.0	46	Aaa
Austin, TX	58	103	30,063	31,488	95.5	42.8	34.6	1.2	48	Aaa
Springfield, MO	58	90	20,612	23,417	88.0	7.7	2.9	2.7	42	Aa2

TABLE 2.23
44 Cities without Suburbs and Almost Cities without Suburbs (continued)

Category	Percentage of urbanized area residents living in city, 2010	City income as percentage of suburban per capita income, 2009	City per capita income, 2005–09 (unadjusted $)	City per capita income, 2005–09 (COL adjusted $)	COL index, 2010	Black and Hispanic percentage of city population, 2010	Black and Hispanic percentage of suburban population, 2010	City:suburb ratio of Black and Hispanic population, 2010 (suburb = 1)	Metro residential segregation index for Blacks, 2010	Moody's bond rating (latest)
Reno, NV	57	89	27,726	27,435	101.1	26.9	21.2	1.3	32	Aa3
Visalia, CA	57	153	23,769	n.a.	n.a.	47.8	67.4	0.7	25	n.r.
Omaha, NW	56	95	26,247	29,725	88.3	26.6	7.8	3.4	58	Aaa
Modesto, CA	56	110	23,266	n.a.	n.a.	39.2	47.8	0.8	31	A3
Spokane, WA	54	89	23,099	24,602	93.9	7.2	5.3	1.4	29	Aa2
Santa Rosa, CA	54	88	30,258	n.a.	n.a.	30.8	23.9	1.3	31	Aa3
Augusta–Richmond, GA	51	83	20,175	21,639	93.2	58.2	29.2	2.0	45	A2
Rockford, IL	51	85	21,757	23,543	92.4	35.8	12.6	2.8	55	Aa3
Evansville, IN	51	81	21,204	22,049	96.2	15.1	4.6	3.3	50	Aa2
29-city average	**59**	**99**	**24,585**	**26,240**	**93.9**	**36**	**22**	**1.6**	**45**	**Aa2**
93 non-cities without suburbs	**28**	**79**	**24,557**	**22,963**	**110.5**	**48.2**	**20.7**	**2.3**	**56**	**A1/Aa3**
56 inelastic-city averages	25	73	23,705	21,195	116.1	51.0	17.7	2.9	61	A1
37 elastic-city averages	33	88	25,847	25,639	102.0	44.0	25.2	1.7	49	Aa2

Note: n.a. = not available; n.r. = not rated; COL = cost of living.

per capita income of city residents must be 90 percent or more of the average per capita income of suburban residents. Below this standard, steady suburbanization of the middle class is typically occurring. San Antonio and Jacksonville, for example, each contain more than 70 percent of their urbanized population; however, average incomes within the two cities are below 90 percent of suburban levels. Third, the city's proportion of Black and Hispanic residents must be no more than three times their proportions in the surrounding suburbs. Beyond this level, the racial and ethnic divides between city dwellers and suburbanites are noticeable. On this basis, Fort Wayne and Wichita, for example, fall short.

By 2010, only nine cities still met all three of my criteria for cities without suburbs (Table 2.23). Two were consolidated governments: Anchorage and Lexington–Fayette. The others maintained their dominance of the local area through aggressive annexation policies.

Thirty-five other cities almost met the criteria. I have labeled them "almost cities without suburbs." Three fell short of the 90 percent income threshold but otherwise qualified. Another three fell short by having disproportionate minority populations compared with their suburbs. Another 29 cities usually met the income and demographic criteria but, by 2010, only housed between 51 percent and 67 percent of their region's urbanized population.

Finally, the performance of the remaining 93 central cities is summarized at the bottom of Table 2.23. I have divided these into inelastic cities and elastic cities. The 37 elastic cities, including such Sun Belt behemoths as Houston, Phoenix, San Diego, and Dallas, had slowly fallen behind the pace of suburbanization.

None of the cities without suburbs or any of their almost-cousins is paradise. None is exempt from the social problems of modern-day America. To the eyes of some residents of the nation's more glamorous and cosmopolitan centers, most of these 44 cities may appear to be modest communities that (in Winston Churchill's words) "have much to be modest about." And yet, both as cities and as whole metro areas, they are doing pretty well. With the notable exception of Anchorage, most have average or below-average costs of living. Thus, their residents' nominal incomes (as reported by the census) stretch further than higher incomes reported in high-cost regions, such as the Boston-to-Washington corridor or Northern and Southern California.

The cities without suburbs and almost-cities without suburbs dominated their urbanized areas in 2010, containing 84 percent and 67 percent, respectively, of their urbanized populations; the other 93 central cities contained only 28 percent. Residents of cities without suburbs might be expected to be better off than residents of less elastic cities that are a smaller share of their regions' populations and where many of the wealthy have fled to their suburbs. In 2009, the residents of cities without suburbs had incomes 7 percent above suburban levels; the residents of almost cities without suburbs were near parity at 97 percent, while in the other 85 cities, average incomes were 21 percent below that of their suburbs.

Adjusted for differences in cost of living, real per capita income translated into $25,632 for residents of cities without suburbs, $26,006 for residents of almost cities without suburbs, and $21,195 for residents of the 56 inelastic cities—a 21 percent higher standard of living for residents of cities without suburbs. The economic strength of these cities was reflected in somewhat better municipal bond ratings (Aa2); none of the 44 cities had less than an A rating (except Stockton).

The key, I believe, is that these 44 communities are becoming societies of greater social equity and economic mobility. They have lower levels of racial segregation—segregation indices of 44 and 47, compared with 61 for the inelastic metro areas—but are still far, however, from being truly integrated societies. Because these regions have greater unity among their public institutions, their residents have better access to their entire region's resources than do residents of more fragmented regions.

In short, however modest cities without suburbs may appear on the world stage, they are making more of their region's available resources. What would happen if more fragmented regions, particularly their inelastic inner cities, could harness the resources and opportunities of their entire regions? Chapter 3 discusses some of the possibilities.

Notes

1. Of the 786 central cities, I was able to locate data on population count and geographic size in 1950 for 685 cities. Another 41 cities either were too small to be contained in the Census Bureau's "Geographic Report: Land Area and Population of Incorporated Places of 2,500 or more: April 1, 1950," (U.S. Bureau of the Census, Washington, DC, 1953) or did not provide the bureau with reliable data regarding their municipal area for that publication (and I could not locate an alternate source of the information on the Internet). In addition, 45 cities were incorporated after 1950, including such very substantial cities as Scottsdale, Arizona (incorporated in 1951; 2010 population 217,385); Fremont (1956; 214,089), Irvine (1971; 212,375), and Lancaster, California (1977; 156,633); Overland Park,

Kansas (1960; 173,372); and Port St. Lucie, Florida (1961; 164,603). Finally, 15 designated "central cities" are simply unincorporated census-designated places (CDPs), which have no municipal existence (though they may be very real in the minds of their residents and the U.S. Postal Service). CDPs include such well-known addresses as Bethesda, Maryland (61,209); Reston, Virginia (58,404); Metairie, Louisiana (138,481); Paradise, Nevada (223,167); and—most surprisingly (as discussed)—Honolulu, Hawaii (390,738).

2.   Nevertheless, to maintain continuity with earlier editions of *Cities without Suburbs*, I did keep Rockford, Illinois (349,341); Savannah, Georgia (347,611); and Ann Arbor, Michigan (344,791) within the group of 163 larger MSAs.

3.   Within the category of central cities of more than 100,000 people, I included nine inelastic cities that formerly had more than 100,000 residents but that have dropped below that level and are still their region's central cities: Albany, New York; Camden, New Jersey; Canton, Ohio; Gary, Indiana; Reading, Pennsylvania; Scranton, Pennsylvania; Trenton, New Jersey; Wilmington, Delaware; and Youngstown, Ohio. Also included are Davenport, Iowa (99,685), and West Palm Beach, Florida (99,919), whose population counts I decided were adequate for the purpose. I also kept the Harrisburg, Pennsylvania, area in the group because its trends were analyzed in Chapter 1. These cities not only illustrated important lessons about relative elasticity and inelasticity, but also their regions averaged more than 675,000 residents in 2010.

4.   In the first edition of *Cities without Suburbs*, I gave equal weight to initial density and boundary expansion. Through further statistical analysis, I found that assigning three times greater importance to boundary expansion better "fit" a central city's capture/contribute percentage. The effect is to emphasize the importance of annexation and city–county consolidation in a city's relative elasticity ranking.

5.   Of 383 metro areas, the only ones to lose population over the 60 years were Pittsfield, Massachusetts (–1 percent); Jersey City, New Jersey, and Pine Bluff, Arkansas (which both dropped –2 percent); and nine steel and coal-mining regions: Danville, Illinois (–6 percent); Charleston, West Virginia, and Cumberland, Maryland–West Virginia (both –8 percent); Pittsburgh and Altoona, Pennsylvania (both –9 percent); Scranton–Wilkes Barre, Pennsylvania (–14 percent); Steubenville–Weirton, Ohio–West Virginia (–21 percent); Wheeling, West Virginia–Ohio (–25 percent); and Johnstown, Pennsylvania (–31 percent).

6.   Birmingham contributed 3 percent of its households to suburban growth. Decades ago, Yankee "little boxism" followed the steel industry south to the Birmingham area. With 34 independent towns and smaller cities organized outside its city limits (representing 42 percent of Jefferson County's population), Birmingham is surrounded by more incorporated, not-very-neighborly suburbs than any other southern city. Of Birmingham's 34 suburban municipalities, 21 have been organized since World War II.

7.   Since 1950, the 19 other household-losing cities were Camden (–29 percent change); Harrisburg (–25 percent); Newark (–22 percent); Dayton (–18 percent); Scranton (–17 percent); Cincinnati (–16 percent); Gary (–16 percent); Flint

(−16 percent); Canton (−15 percent); New Orleans (−14 percent); Providence (−13 percent); Hartford (−12 percent); Trenton (−11 percent); Syracuse (−10 percent); Wilmington, Delaware (−9 percent); Rochester −8 percent); Baltimore (−7 percent); Reading (−7 percent); and Chicago (−4 percent).

8.   Particularly striking as rapidly gentrifying cities were Atlanta (a city household size of 2.27 compared to a suburban household size of 2.77); Washington, D.C. (2.26 compared to 2.75); Seattle (2.15 compared to 2.63); Denver (2.28 to 2.62); and San Francisco (2.33 compared to 2.69).

9.   Examples would be Paterson (3.30 persons per household in the city compared to 2.81 in the suburbs), Camden (3.16 compared to 2.68), Reading (2.94 compared to 2.60), Providence (2.84 compared to 2.52), and Hartford (2.77 compared to 2.54).

10.   In 1970, the average Black segregation index was 80.4 for 29 inelastic metro areas and 79.8 for 12 elastic metro areas (most metro areas with somewhat smaller geographies).

11.   The five metro areas where Black segregation increased were Manchester, New Hampshire; Ann Arbor, Michigan; Madison, Wisconsin; Vallejo–Fairfield, California; and Anchorage, Alaska. Collectively, they had relatively small Black populations in 1980 (averaging 5.9 percent), by 2010 had experienced substantial Black population growth (to 8.8 percent), and had a relatively low segregation rate in 1980 (averaging 41.5) that increased modestly (averaging 44.1) in 2010.

12.   Group A included Raleigh, Charlotte, Durham, Winston-Salem, Greensboro, and Wilmington (all in North Carolina); Atlanta; Orlando; Nashville; Lexington; Indianapolis; and Provo. The exception was the Scranton–Wilkes Barre region, which probably experienced substantial domestic migration from the New York–Northern New Jersey and Philadelphia areas.

13.   In addition to Corpus Christi, Group F members were Albuquerque; Tucson; Miami; San Antonio; and Los Angeles, Oxnard, Bakersfield, Salinas, Fresno, and Anaheim–Santa Ana (all in California). The exception was Jersey City, which lies across the Hudson River from New York City.

14.   Group C included Detroit and Lansing as well as Flint in Michigan; Akron, Canton, Cleveland, Dayton, Toledo, and Youngstown in Ohio; Rochester and Buffalo (western New York); Pittsburgh and Philadelphia; St. Louis; Peoria; and Davenport.

15.   Table 2.10 uses the same combined dissimilarity indices measuring the segregation of the poor and the segregation of the affluent used in Table 1.14 and discussed in note 13 of Chapter 1.

16.   The regions where economic segregation diminished were medium-elasticity Atlanta, Baton Rouge, and Wilmington (North Carolina); high-elasticity Chattanooga, Jackson, Columbia, Winston-Salem, and Springfield (Missouri); and hyper-elasticity Raleigh, Lexington, Huntsville, and Charlotte. Though classified as a zero-elasticity metro area, Wilmington, Delaware, was also located in a legally segregated state subject to the U.S. Supreme Court's *Brown v. Board of Education* desegregation ruling.

17. The fair share of poverty index is explained in Lesson 19 in Chapter 1.

18. As a single-county region in 1990 with just two small villages in addition to the dominant city (80 percent of Bernalillo County's population), metro Albuquerque's MPDI was 2.03 in 1992.

19. Of 137 metro areas, from 1969 to 2009, the relative share of manufacturing jobs increased fractionally only in Vallejo–Fairfield, California (5.06 percent to 5.47 percent), and Reno–Sparks, Nevada (4.72 percent to 4.77 percent). Undoubtedly, they will be joined by a handful of other areas as manufacturing revives after the Great Recession.

20. Harvey B. Gantt, "A Tale of Two Cities: Charlotte's Regional Approach Means Fast Decisions, Fast Results," in "Turning Point," a special section of the *Boston Globe*, October 30, 1994, 28.

21. For example, in 2008, the cost of living in the zero-elasticity San Francisco region (an index of 164) was almost twice the cost of living in the high-elasticity Indianapolis region (87). The principal difference was the cost of housing, which was almost four times higher in the San Francisco region (an index of 281) than in the Indianapolis region (73).

22. Receiving Aaa ratings were Portland (Oregon), Denver, Omaha, Madison, Columbus, Salt Lake City, San Antonio, Huntsville, Austin, and Oklahoma City, as well as North Carolina's I-85 quintet (Raleigh, Durham, Greensboro, Winston-Salem, and Charlotte).

23. The downgraded cities (italicized in the tables) are East St. Louis, North Chicago, and Chicago Heights, Illinois; East Chicago and Hammond, Indiana; Holyoke, Massachusetts; McKeesport, Easton, Norristown, and Sharon, Pennsylvania; Paterson and Elizabeth, New Jersey; and Alliance, Ohio.

Chapter 3

Strategies for Stretching Cities

Reversing the fragmentation of urban areas is an essential step in ending severe racial and economic segregation. The "city" must be redefined to reunify city and suburb.

Optimally, such reunification is achieved through formally organizing a metropolitan or quasi-metropolitan government (a "Big Box"). In smaller, single-county regions, it can be accomplished through formal city–county consolidation, which is, in effect, a type of superannexation by the central city. Steady annexation by the central city can serve much the same goal.

Where city–county consolidation cannot be achieved (which will be in most regions) or annexation is either impossible or becoming more difficult, three key policies must be implemented so that the many little boxes will act as a Big Box. Such functional policies may be termed "elasticity mimics."[1]

Three Essential Regional Policies

A city and suburb would be reunified if a metro government adopted (or multiple local governments were required to adopt by state government) three policies:

- Implement regional inclusionary zoning and other mixed-income housing strategies for integrating low-income households into middle-class communities to diminish racial and economic segregation and eliminate concentrated poverty.
- Implement regional land use and transportation planning and growth management strategies to control suburban sprawl and reverse urban disinvestment.

- Implement regional tax-base sharing to reduce fiscal imbalances that result from uneven growth and socioeconomic imbalances.

Tax-base sharing alone would be inadequate; no feasible amount of money can salvage isolated inner cities and declining inner suburbs. Unfettered urban sprawl promotes economic segregation and constantly threatens inelastic cities and older suburbs with slow abandonment. Fair-share housing programs are slow to take hold and are

---

Box 3.1 Montgomery County: Mixing Up the Neighborhood

Montgomery County, Maryland, has long been renowned as having the nation's most progressive mixed-income housing policies. The Housing Opportunities Commission (the county's public housing authority and housing finance agency) owns, rents, or administers an inventory of more than 44,000 housing units (most in mixed-income neighborhoods), or about 12 percent of the total housing supply.

One of Montgomery County's key tools is its Moderately Priced Dwelling Unit (MPDU) ordinance. Enacted in 1973, the MPDU law requires private developers to build mixed-income housing everywhere. The law now covers any new subdivision, townhouse complex, or apartment development with at least 20 housing units.

Under the county law, most of the new housing can be market rate (at whatever income level the builder targets), but at least 12.5 to 15.0 percent must be affordable housing, or MPDUs. To offset builders' costs, the MPDU law provides up to a 22 percent density bonus that covers both MPDU land costs and permits construction of additional market-rate units. To qualify for an MPDU, a family's income cannot exceed 65 percent of the county's median household income (which was $114,600 in 2011 for a four-person household).

To help integrate the poorest households into middle-class society, the county law further specifies that one-third of the MPDUs, or 5 percent of the total units built in a subdivision, must be available for rent or outright purchase by the Housing Opportunities Commission. Montgomery County never builds public housing projects. It simply buys standard housing scattered all over the county as rental housing for its poorest families.

Complying with the county's ground rules, private homebuilders and apartment developers by 2010 produced 13,133 MPDUs—70 percent for sale, 30 percent for rent. Many buyers are local schoolteachers, county deputy sheriffs, office workers, supermarket clerks, and fast-food cooks—in short, the very civil servants,

most effective within a vigorously expanding housing market. All three strategies are inseparable and indispensable parts of a successful approach.

DIMINISH RACIAL AND ECONOMIC SEGREGATION

"Public policy dictates where development occurs," states the National Association of Home Builders (surely no champions of gov-

---

retail trade workers, and service industry workers who serve local communities.

To house welfare recipients and other poor residents, the Housing Opportunities Commission has purchased more than 1,700 of the new MPDUs and rents 1,200 more. (Church groups and private nonprofits have bought others.) The county-owned units are so scattered that the commission pays annual membership assessments to more than 220 private homeowners' associations.

The 85-10-5 income mix produces no social problems, according to Housing Opportunities Commission officials, police, and social agencies, and resale prices of market-rate homes are unaffected by being within mixed-income housing developments.

With 972,000 residents in 2010, Montgomery County is a governmental Big Box. In 1927, the Maryland General Assembly gave the county government almost exclusive planning and zoning control throughout the county.[a]

The county's progressive policies have produced a remarkable social and economic transformation. In 1970, Montgomery County had the look of a classic suburb—wealthy and White (92 percent). By 2010, Montgomery County had a "rainbow look"—16.6 percent Black, 17.0 percent Hispanic, 13.9 percent Asian, and 3.2 percent mixed race and other—and was still the 11th-wealthiest county in America while becoming one of the nation's more racially and economically integrated communities.

By providing housing for all occupational levels, the county helped promote a diversified local economy centered on its Interstate 270 "Technology Corridor." In a generation, Montgomery County has become the global center of biomedical and genetic research.

a. The legislature grandfathered existing zoning powers for the cities of Rockville and Gaithersburg and five small villages (about 12 percent of the county's population).

ernmental regulation). Through planning and zoning powers, local governments shape what gets built where for whose benefit, affecting, in particular, the local housing market. A broad-based Big Box government is not generally as afflicted with the NIMBY (not in my backyard) syndrome as is a narrow-based, little boxes government. A Big Box can carry out inclusionary zoning policies that require private, for-profit homebuilders to create mixed-income rather than economically segregated housing developments (see Box 3.1). Also, within its wide jurisdiction, a Big Box can scatter public housing projects and implement rent subsidy programs across many neighborhoods.

That a Big Box would automatically pursue such policies is hardly guaranteed. Nevertheless, it can and does happen. In a highly fragmented metro area, however, the many little boxes will not adopt such politically controversial policies without being compelled to do so by state legislatures or state courts.

CONTROL SUBURBAN SPRAWL

Suburban sprawl doesn't just happen as the natural outcome of some unfettered free market forces. Sprawl is the result of an interlocking complex of federal, state, and local policies that set the framework for private investment. Most state legislatures have delegated broad planning and zoning powers to local governments to regulate land development. *If it has the political will*, a Big Box can promote more compact development, preserve farmland and natural areas, and encourage reinvestment in older residential and commercial areas (see Box 3.2). Within a little boxes region, for one little box to undertake such policies by itself is virtually useless (and even perilous). Once again, getting all neighboring little boxes to act as one invariably requires state mandates or very powerful state (or federal) incentives.

REDUCE FISCAL IMBALANCE

By taxing a larger share of a region's wealth, a Big Box matches resources to problems. A Big Box is implicitly a tax-base-sharing mechanism; it taxes richer neighborhoods to maintain adequate services in poorer neighborhoods that could not afford to pay for such services by themselves. In little boxes regions, however, richer and poorer neighborhoods are separate governments unto themselves. Poorer communities have no way of tapping the wealth of richer communities without the intervention of a higher level of government (see Box 3.3).

Metro Government: A Definition

Before examining the feasibility of creating metro governments, I need to offer a working definition of what a metro government is. The country abounds with more than 37,000 special-purpose units of local government (transit authorities, water and sewer agencies, and community college districts, for example). Often they are metro-wide. Although creating special-purpose governments may be seen as a step toward ultimately achieving metropolitan unification, a true metro government must be a general-purpose local government. It must have all the powers of a municipality under applicable state law. Moreover, it must exercise exclusive powers over its responsibilities within its jurisdiction. In other words, it must not be a general government that just fills in the interstices between a myriad of major municipal enclaves. Such is the situation of many county governments regarding unincorporated land in highly urbanized areas.

A metro government need not be responsible for all local public functions. Special-purpose and other local general governments can still exist. *A metro government, however, must control key planning and zoning powers and housing policy.*

Though preferable, a metro government need not cover the entire metro area; it should contain at least 60 percent of the metro area's population (or 70 percent of the urbanized area's population) and have within its jurisdiction a substantial amount of undeveloped land. Thus, it can either control much new peripheral development or pursue land conservation policies, promoting more compact development. A metro government must include the region's central city.

State Government's Crucial Role

Although this book is written from Washington, D.C., it is based on my experiences as a mayor and state legislator. Restructuring local governance is not a national government task. It is primarily the responsibility of citizens and political leaders at the local and state levels. State government sets the rules of the game.

America is a *federal* system. Within the bounds of our national constitution, states have certain sovereign powers. Our national constitution is silent on the topic of local government. Under the Tenth Amendment, authority over local government is implicitly reserved to state governments. Local governments (including local school

Box 3.2 Metro Builds Great Wall of Portland

With its urban growth boundary (UGB), the Portland region has the most effective—and unique—integrated system of transportation and land use planning in the United States.

Its effectiveness is based on the state of Oregon's Land Use Act of 1973, which required Oregon's 36 county governments to adopt sprawl-limiting, comprehensive land use plans that comply with 14 state goals. The county plans incorporate UGBs for Oregon's 242 municipalities that clearly divide urban from rural land.

Its uniqueness rests in the fact that, for the complex, highly urbanized Portland region, Portland Metro—the country's only directly elected regional government—is the regional planning agency. Metro is governed by a president elected region-wide and a six-member council elected directly from the six districts into which the region is divided. (None can be elected officials of other governments.) They, in turn, hire a professional chief operating officer.

Metro is not an all-purpose government. It does not replace the 3 county and 24 municipal governments within its region. Metro is a special-purpose government that was established by the Oregon legislature and the region's voters explicitly to be the regional planning agency.

Periodically, Metro has been assigned responsibility for certain regional services, such as the Oregon Zoo, the Oregon Convention Center, the Portland Center for the Performing Arts, the regional parks system, and a regional solid waste disposal and recycling system. These are major functions in terms of Metro's current $385 million budget and 752 full-time employees in fiscal year 2011/12. However, they are minor functions compared with Metro's planning powers to shape the region's future.

Adopted in 1979, the regional UGB originally contained 342 square miles. The UGB draws a clear line between two types of areas:

- Land preserved exclusively for farming, forestry, and wilderness and recreation areas (no urbanization allowed)
- Land that would be urbanized

Inside the UGB, sufficient land must be provided for 20 years of anticipated residential, commercial, and industrial growth. (As a

districts) are legally creatures of state government. State legislatures frame the standards and procedures by which new municipalities are created. Typically, state governments can do more than merely set the ground rules for local action. State legislatures can also cre-

result, Metro has expanded the UGB six times in 32 years, adding a total of 60 square miles to the UGB.)

In 2010, more than 1.42 million people (over 85 percent of the population of the three-county region) lived within the 402-square-mile UGB. The rest of the population lived in smaller towns and rural areas in the remaining 2,608 square miles outside the UGB.

One measure of the UGB's effectiveness is its success in protecting farmland. During the 1990s, for example, the region's population grew 17.6 percent, but only 0.1 percent of its farmland was urbanized. Planning ahead, Metro expects that a 50 percent increase in population by 2040 will require urbanization of only about 2,500 acres of current farmland.

Another measure of the UGB's effectiveness is the region's balanced economic and social health. By preventing new development from occurring outward, the UGB focuses much private investment inward to the central city and older suburbs. The Portland region is one of the least ethnically and economically segregated societies in the United States. The city of Portland is a growing, Aaa-credit-rated central city. And none of Portland's 23 suburban municipalities is fiscally or socially distressed.

Winston Churchill once said, "We first shape our buildings. Then our buildings shape us." For 30 years, Oregonians have been shaping their building—through the Oregon Land Use Act, state oversight agencies, and Portland Metro. More than a dozen times since 1978, voters of the region have gone to the polls to elect the Metro Council or amend Metro's charter. Land use and transportation planning controversies are always the election issues.

Beyond the government institutions, Oregon has developed a powerful citizens lobby, 1,000 Friends of Oregon. Serving as a watchdog over the entire process, 1,000 Friends of Oregon has many times defended good planning principles and citizens' right to be involved in planning decisions.

That intensely democratic process has, in turn, reshaped the builders. Oregon has broader and more knowledgeable citizen involvement in land use planning issues (particularly, within Portland Metro communities) than has any other area of the United States.

To the extent that Oregonians are different, their institutions have helped to educate and shape them.

ate new local governments and merge old ones (including school districts)—often without any constitutional requirement for local voter approval. However, after consolidating more than 108,000 local school districts (as of 1942) into fewer than 16,000 larger, more

---

Box 3.3 Twin Cities Region Shares Tax Base

The Mall of America, the biggest mall in the United States, sits in suburban Bloomington, Minnesota. Yet every one of 186 municipalities and more than 100 school districts and special authorities in the seven-county Minneapolis–St. Paul region shares in the millions of dollars in tax revenues generated by the giant mall.

Why? The Twin Cities' Fiscal Disparities Plan, the nation's largest regional tax-base-sharing program.

Enacted in 1971 by the Minnesota legislature, the plan pools 40 percent of the increase in all communities' commercial and industrial property valuations. All cities and townships keep their pre-1971 tax bases plus 60 percent of the annual growth. The pool is then taxed at a uniform rate and redistributed among all local government entities.

The redistribution formula estimates each community's annual population and how its commercial and industrial tax base per capita compares with the regional per capita average. Poorer-than-

---

unified districts (by 1972), legislatures have rarely exercised such powers since.[2]

Furthermore, governors and state legislators can and do act as metro-wide policy makers. State governments have mandated area-wide local cooperation in a wide range of functional activities (transportation planning, sewage treatment, air quality control, senior citizens programs) or (much more rarely) regional tax-base sharing or fair-share affordable housing programs.

State government also plays an increasingly important role in providing state aid for local government and, above all, for local school systems. By 2009, state aid had grown to 20 percent of city and county government revenues. By the 2007–08 school year, state governments were providing 48 percent of local school districts' budgets. With the purse comes additional power (and responsibility) to provide for the more rational and equitable organization of metro areas.

Statutory authority aside, however, why should governors and state legislators have any greater political opportunity to implement unpopular reforms? Are they not elected by the same voters as local officials?

Governors, of course, have statewide constituencies, and most state legislative districts are not coterminous with local government

average communities receive more back from the fund than they contribute. Richer-than-average communities contribute more than they receive.

By 2011, the annual Fiscal Disparities Fund amounted to $544 million, over 39 percent of all commercial and industrial property taxes collected. Some 120 municipalities were net recipients; 60 were net contributors. The net contributors were primarily wealthy suburbs lying in the "Fertile Crescent" southwest of the Twin Cities. Giant malls, office towers, and gardenlike industrial parks have sprouted along the interstate highways that border these suburbs or adjacent to the suburban Minneapolis–St. Paul International Airport.

The tax-base-sharing program narrows fiscal disparities between rich and poor communities. Without the plan, the disparity in tax base per capita among cities with more than 10,000 residents would be 10 to 1. The Fiscal Disparities Plan narrows the gap to 3 to 1 between richest and poorest.

jurisdictions. Moreover, there is a tendency to view central cities and suburbs as monolithic blocks automatically opposed to each other. (This book is seemingly guilty of that perspective.) In reality, tremendous variety exists among both central cities (which I have tried to illustrate) and suburban communities.

Suburban diversity is the key to building effective political coalitions in state legislatures. Both inelastic central cities and older, often blue-collar suburbs are victimized by typical regional growth patterns that focus most high-end residential and commercial development in newer suburbs. Indeed, when "inner-city" problems begin to grow rapidly in older, blue-collar suburbs, these communities often have fewer resources to combat rising poverty, crime, and other problems than have central cities. Central cities and older suburbs are potentially allied by mutual self-interest, and the state legislature is the arena in which bonds can be forged (see Box 3.4).

TOWNSHIP STATES VS. COUNTY STATES

How local governance is organized in different states has a big impact on central city elasticity and on the degree to which city–county consolidation and annexation are feasible strategies. The six states of New England plus New York, New Jersey, and Pennsylvania are completely divided into incorporated cities, boroughs or villages, and towns (see Box 3.5). No unincorporated land is available for their cities to annex. Most midwestern states are also totally divided into townships, but a township's legal status varies from state to state. In recent decades, Michigan townships, for example, have wielded strong political power; most have resisted annexation successfully. By contrast, townships in Indiana exist largely to tax local property owners for indigent relief and play no role in annexation decisions. A band of 20 "township states" (that is, little boxes states) extends north of the Mason–Dixon line and of the Ohio River from Maine to North Dakota.

The rest of the country is made up of "county states" (or Big Box states), where urbanized islands exist as incorporated cities, towns,

---

Box 3.4 *Metropolitics*: The United States in Red, Orange, and Blue

"We're spending too much time flirting with Blue Land," the community organizer said in a staff meeting. "We need to do more hard, grassroots organizing in Orange Land to add to our base in Red Land."

Blue Land? Red Land? *Orange* Land? This is not some variation on network television's election night coverage. It is a new tool for understanding metropolitan America—multicolored maps.

The maps are the creation of Myron Orfield. Now a full-time champion of regionalism, as a Minnesota legislator Orfield forged the first enduring alliance in America between declining central cities and older, threatened blue-collar suburbs.

Orfield also pioneered the use of a political tool: maps that, jurisdiction by jurisdiction, trace the decline of central cities (colored red) and many older inner-ring suburbs (colored orange) and mark the rise of affluent outer-ring suburbs (colored blue).

He told this story first in *Metropolitics: A Regional Agenda for Community and Stability*.[a] Through the work of his Ameregis Corporation, Orfield has now mapped dozens of metropolitan regions, spreading his doctrine of "metropolitics." His work in the 25 largest metropolitan areas is summarized in *American Metropolitics: The New Suburban Reality*.[b] His most in-depth analysis is *Region: Planning the Future of the Twin Cities*.[c]

A few academicians and journalists had pointed out how urban poverty was spreading from the inner city to the inner suburbs, but Orfield has developed the most compelling and comprehen-

and villages in the midst of a sea of unincorporated land. For unincorporated areas, county government serves as a kind of general-purpose government, though it typically offers a less intensive level of services than would a municipal government. With the exception of Virginia's system of independent cities, municipal annexation does not remove an area from a county's overall jurisdiction, so county governments often support municipal annexations.

Encourage City–County Consolidation

Typically, movements to create area-wide government units have focused on consolidating municipal governments with their surrounding county governments. In recent decades, the most notable consolida-

---

sive documentation of this trend and has translated it into effective political action.

Metropolitics teaches that making progress on hard, divisive issues such as controlling sprawl, creating mixed-income housing, or sharing tax bases is rarely based on friendly, consensual agreement, but more often on the building of political coalitions. In highly fragmented little boxes regions, only state legislatures can serve as regional policy bodies, setting new ground rules for how myriad local governments must share common responsibilities for common problems. Those coalitions are most durable when based on each member's political self-interest. The glue that held the Minnesota legislative coalition together was underlying social, economic, and political self-interest.

Orfield's maps graphically portray that underlying self-interest, getting city and suburban politicians to see beyond traditional racial division and history to a common agenda. The emerging central city–older suburbs alliance is America's best hope for changing the rules of the game.

a. Myron Orfield, *Metropolitics: A Regional Agenda for Community and Stability* (Washington, DC: Brookings Institution Press, 1997).

b. Myron Orfield, *American Metropolitics: The New Suburban Reality* (Washington, DC: Brookings Institution Press, 2002).

c. Myron Orfield and Thomas F. Luce Jr., *Region: Planning the Future of the Twin Cities* (Minneapolis: University of Minnesota Press, 2010).

Box 3.5 Northern-Tier States Fragmented by Townships

There are 16,519 townships recorded in the 2007 Census of Governments, covering 20 northern states. In New England, New York, New Jersey, and Pennsylvania, towns and townships originated in colonial times. But why does this system exist in most of the Midwest? Blame it on Thomas Hutchins.

Thomas Hutchins was a New Jersey–born engineering captain in the Royal American or 60th Regiment of Foot of the British Army stationed at Fort Pitt (Pittsburgh) at the end of the French and Indian War in 1764. Hutchins proposed surveying the vast Ohio Territory, which had come to victorious England from defeated France. He would divide the wilderness into townships 6 miles square and further subdivide townships into 160-acre sections. British army veterans would be allotted sections of western lands as a reward for their military service.

Nothing came immediately of Hutchins's plan, but Hutchins threw in his lot with the rebellious colonists a decade later, becoming Geographer General of the Americans' Southern Army. At the end of the War for Independence, the Continental Congress (under the Articles of Confederation) adopted Hutchins's plan as the Land Ordinance of 1785 and appointed him first Geographer of the United States to implement it. Congress's motivation was the same as Hutchins's original intent: pay off veterans of the Continental Army with western lands. (The biggest beneficiary was General George Washington, who claimed 23,333 acres near the future Columbus, Ohio.) As the different territories (Ohio, Indiana, Michigan, and so on) became states, their constitutions converted "congressional townships" into local units of government.

Whatever these townships' value was in civilizing the 19th-century frontier, in the 21st century the overall effect is the atomization of local governance. With 2,642 local general governments, for example, Minnesota has one government for every 1,948 residents. With 1,299 cities and villages and 1,432 townships (not to mention 912 independent school districts and another 3,249 special districts), Illinois is the champion of microgovernment.

The New England town meeting is enshrined in the American myth, and the National Association of Towns and Townships proudly proclaims itself the champion of "hometown government" and "grassroots government." However, township states, or little boxes states, contain most of the country's most racially and economically segregated metro areas, and local communities' ability to compete economically is constantly constrained by the absence of governance structures to pull together regional resources.

tions have merged the central city with single counties. Indianapolis–Marion County, Nashville–Davidson County, Jacksonville–Duval County, and Louisville–Jefferson County are examples. (See Box 3.6 for more 19th-century examples in addition to New York City.)

Each city–county consolidation has been (and must be) custom-made for its area. The final structure should represent a compromise, balancing good government idealism, tradition, and political realities. Traditional functions of county government may be absorbed into the newly unified government (Nashville–Davidson) or may be continued as independent functions while the new government assumes service-providing functions for all unincorporated areas (Indianapolis–Marion County). Bowing to political reality, certain municipal enclaves may remain in existence (for example, Baldwin and the three "Beaches" within Jacksonville–Duval County), and

---

Box 3.6 Whatever Happened to the City of Spring Garden?

What ever happened to Spring Garden, Northern Liberties, Kensington, Southwark, and Moyamensing? In 1850, these Pennsylvania communities were the 9th, 11th, 12th, 20th, and 28th most populous cities in America. Four years later they were consolidated with the larger city of Philadelphia and unincorporated areas of Philadelphia County to frame the boundaries of the city of Philadelphia as we know it today.

In fact, 10 of the country's 50 largest cities in 1850 disappeared before 1900. They all were consolidated into larger government bodies.

In 1867, Boston annexed the city of Roxbury; seven years later it leaped across Boston harbor to annex the city of Charlestown. Allegheny, in 1907, was taken in by Pittsburgh. And in the tradition of "little fish–big fish–bigger fish," the 24th-largest city in 1850, Williamsburg, was annexed in 1854 by the city of Brooklyn (7th largest), which in turn became part of New York City in 1898 (revisit Box 1.2).

The political geography of mature metropolitan areas may appear immutable to their residents today, but more than a century ago compelling public interests were served by such consolidations. Popular opposition as well as natural obstacles (harbors and rivers) had to be overcome, but the effort was worthwhile. These new government structures served their communities well for many decades.

rural residents may have to be assured that consolidation will not mean an automatic increase in taxes through maintaining a lower-service, lower-tax zone (Nashville's General Services District).

Despite such compromises, most city–county consolidations do initially achieve the key goals of adding more developable land, more people, and a higher tax base to the central city. In effect, the current population, the tax base, and an inventory of undeveloped land in unincorporated areas constitute a "dowry" that county government brings to the marriage with the city.

Absent such elastic effects, however, consolidation just eliminates one level of government. That was the result when Kansas City, Kansas, having previously annexed all remaining land within Wyandotte County, consolidated with what had become a redundant county government. Similarly, in little boxes New York State, consolidating Rochester with Monroe County or Buffalo with Erie County, for instance, would have no city-stretching effects. None of Rochester's 29 nor Buffalo's 42 neighboring cities and towns would likely consolidate into the new entity. The two cities would be swapping their elected mayors and city councils for elected county executives and county legislatures with little or no net increase in resources for the central cities.

I cannot emphasize this point enough. Of the 33 post–World War II city–county consolidations, all but one (Indianapolis–Marion County) occurred in Big Box states. Furthermore, in eight of them, smaller incorporated cities, towns, and villages were also present. Not one smaller municipality joined in the consolidation. Not one … anywhere … ever. (Revisit Box 1.3 on Louisville–Jefferson County.)

With the continued spread of suburbia and long-distance commuting, the consolidated cities' long-term dilemma is that metro areas steadily grow beyond their new boundaries. Indianapolis–Marion County, Nashville–Davidson County, and Jacksonville–Duval County were all highly successful consolidations of the 1960s. At the time of their consolidation Nashville–Davidson County was 92 percent of its three-county metro area's population; Indianapolis–Marion County was 70 percent of its eight-county area; and Jacksonville–Duval County was 95 percent of its single-county area. Today, Nashville–Davidson County's population is only 38 percent of its 13-county area; Indianapolis-Marion County, only 47 percent of its 10-county metro area; and Jacksonville-Duval County, 61 percent of its 5-county area.

To maintain city–county consolidation's benefits, these multi-county regions must now adopt strong anti-sprawl growth management policies.

Potential impact of city–county consolidation

City–county consolidations have been relatively rare—as stated, only 33 since World War II. In fact, only 19 states have specific statutes authorizing city–county consolidation and setting forth the procedures for its achievement (Table 3.1). Of the 19 states, 7 are in the West, 8 in the South, 4 in the Midwest, and none in the Northeast, where counties often hardly exist as meaningful governmental units. Of the 19 states, 16 require various forms of local referenda. (The exceptions are California, Utah, and Virginia.)

The absence of authorizing legislation, however, does not preclude most legislatures from implementing specific city–county consolidations as legislative acts. Such, indeed, was the path followed successfully in consolidating Indianapolis–Marion County as well as, a century ago, in creating New York City (revisit Box 1.2).

Table 3.2 projects what might be the hypothetical impact of city–county consolidation. It divides the country into five groups. In Group 0, city–county consolidations are impossible or, rather, highly

TABLE 3.1
STATE LAWS REGARDING CITY–COUNTY CONSOLIDATION

	Number of states				
State law	South (16)	West (13)	Midwest (12)	Northeast (9)	U.S. total (50)
Consolidation of cities and counties is authorized	8	7	4	0	19
Referendum and majority approval of each city affected are required	2	3	2	0	7
Referendum and majority approval of county are required	4	3	0	0	7
Referendum and majority approval of unincorporated area of county are required	1	0	1	0	7

unlikely to occur (at least in my lifetime or, for that matter, in the lifetimes of my grandchildren). This group includes 49 metro areas in New England, New York, New Jersey, and Pennsylvania; 11 independent cities that exist separate and apart from adjacent counties;[3] and 14 large cities that are now totally surrounded by incorporated suburban municipalities.[4] City–county consolidation is improbable for 46 Group 1 metro areas in five strong, midwestern township states. City–county consolidation is at least conceivable for 94 Group 2 metro areas in 16 states that have weak townships or no townships at all.[5] Group 3 contains 148 metro areas in 18 states where such consolidations are possible because workable state city–county consolidation laws are in place, and in 7 of the states, city–county consolidation has actually happened in recent decades.[6] Finally, group 4 contains 20 already consolidated city–counties that are the central cities of their metropolitan areas.[7]

Overall, in 2010, principal central cities housed 32 percent of their regional populations. City–county consolidation would merge the land and population of unincorporated areas with the central city. The consolidated governments' share of metropolitan population would rise to 53 percent. By my definition (that is, the central city contains over 60 percent of the region's population), 34 metropolitan governments existed in 2010. City–county consolidation would raise the number to 193—over half of all metro areas. Most important, consolidation would give the central city effective control over most undeveloped land within the central county.

State action to facilitate consolidation

Uniform state laws should be enacted to encourage city–county consolidation. The desirable provisions of such laws would include the following:

- Establishing a consolidation charter commission by action of city or county government or both
- Authorizing the creation of urban and rural service districts (with different tax levels) within a consolidated government
- Authorizing the inclusion of traditional county functions (sheriff, assessor, clerk, and so on) in the consolidated government
- Authorizing municipalities smaller than the central city to maintain their independent existence while receiving county-type services from the consolidated government, unless they voluntarily join the merger

TABLE 3.2
CITY–COUNTY CONSOLIDATION POTENTIAL

Central cities/metro areas	Number of metro areas	Metro population, 2010	Central city population as percentage of metro population		Number of metro governments	
			Preconsolidation, 2010	Postconsolidation, 2010	Preconsolidation	Postconsolidation
Group 0 (consolidation impossible)	74	92,878,129	21	21	0	0
0.1 cities in "hard" little boxes states	49	29,996,697	19	19	0	0
0.2 "independent" cities	11	15,171,196	24	24	0	0
0.3 "surrounded" cities	14	47,710,236	23	23	0	0
Group 1 (consolidation improbable)	46	12,690,771	33	63	1	27
Group 2 (consolidation conceivable)	94	43,010,332	43	63	14	56
Group 3 (consolidation possible)	148	74,215,137	34	68	12	103
Group 4 (already consolidated)	20	33,749,801	48	48	7	7
Totals	**382**	**256,544,170**	**32**	**53**	**34**	**193**

Note: As a central city–less metro area, Nassau–Suffolk, NY, is omitted.

- Authorizing approval of the consolidated government by a single, county-wide referendum of all affected voters (that is, no single-jurisdiction veto)

As a practical matter, voters have rejected almost three of four city–county consolidation proposals. The fault has rarely been in some design flaw in the proposed form of government. Rejection of consolidation proposals usually reflects either general conservatism about changing "the devil we know for the devil we don't know" or strong opposition by those living outside the central city (that is, "county voters"). County voters typically fear increased taxes or loss of their identity, or they simply want no part of city problems.

Appendix A lists all city–county consolidations since the city of New Orleans merged with Orleans Parish in 1805. Appendix B provides a more select list of potential city–county consolidations than are hypothetically projected in Table 3.2. These 76 communities are ones where the central city is currently 60 percent or more of the county's population—a demographic threshold that seems

---

Box 3.7 Unigov Propels Indianapolis to Big League Status

On a wintry midnight in January 1983, big vans began moving the National Football League's Baltimore Colts to Indianapolis. This dark night will live in infamy for Baltimore civic boosters, but it announced to the world that Indianapolis had arrived in "the bigs."

The crucial step toward acquiring a professional football team was probably taken on January 1, 1970, when "Unigov" came into existence. The consolidation of the city of Indianapolis and Marion County by legislative act was the first consolidation to occur without a popular referendum since New York City was created in 1898.

The legislature's action originated with the Greater Indianapolis Progress Committee's Task Force on Government Structure. Appointed by Richard Lugar (then mayor and later a U.S. senator), the task force of civic, business, and government leaders drafted an 86-page bill modeled in part on the Jacksonville and Nashville consolidations. The task force (ostensibly) then lobbied it through the legislature at a moment when Republicans controlled every key level of local and state government.

"Unigov" was something of a misnomer. Three smaller municipalities, 11 townships, and separate hospital and airport authorities were left unconsolidated. A dozen county constitutional offices

historically to be a precondition for most successful consolidation referenda. Nevertheless, among the 27 "best bets," in the 12 communities in which consolidation proposals have already gone to referenda, voters have rejected consolidation 25 times.

To have widespread impact, unifying local government in metro areas is primarily a task for state government. Too many obstacles exist at the local level, including entrenched officeholders, to rely on local initiative. For reforms to occur on a widespread scale, action must be taken by farsighted and politically courageous governors and legislators. Nineteenth-century legislators frequently took action; 20th-century legislators, rarely (see Box 3.7). What story will the 21st century tell?

IMPROVE ANNEXATION POWERS

In general, Table 3.2 also summarizes the relative potential of central cities in different regions to expand through annexation. Although city–county consolidations are rare, municipal annexations are com-

---

were continued, including the office of Marion County sheriff. Public education was left in 11 separate school districts, bolstering more racial segregation than characterizes many other consolidated communities (with unified, county-wide school districts). Indeed, many in Indianapolis's Black community felt Unigov was designed to dilute the emerging, generally Democratic-voting power of Blacks. (Unigov did not elect a Democratic mayor until 1999.)

Consolidation, however, instantly reenergized Indianapolis, expanding its tax base and cementing a blue-chip municipal bond rating. Lugar's successor as mayor, William Hudnut, praised Unigov: "It brought better delivery of services and lower taxes—taxes that don't go up as fast. Equally important, consolidation has created a wider sense of community that helps you sell your city."[a] In selling their city, Unigov and the business community set out to promote Indianapolis as becoming a major, year-round sports venue.

On New Year's Day, 1970, Baltimore should have "heard footsteps."

a. "Group Hears Indianapolis Mayor Laud Consolidation," *Albuquerque Journal*, March 2, 1991.

mon. During the 2000s, of an estimated 563 central cities that could annex, 501 did.[8] Collectively, in just one decade they expanded their municipal territory from 21,622 square miles to 24,590 square miles—about a 14 percent increase, or almost 3,000 square miles (a land area about 50 percent larger than the entire land area of the state of Delaware). Though most annexations occurred in the South and West, five dozen cities in semi-soft township states succeeded in annexing a square mile or more of land during the decade.

Moreover, this tabulation focuses just on municipalities designated as current (or past) central cities by the federal government. I have tabulated annexation during the past decade for *all* municipalities in three representative states:

- Though still on the books, annexation laws in Michigan, a semi-hard township state, are practically dead letters. According to Census Bureau statistics, from 2000 to 2010, only seven Michigan municipalities (including Lansing and East Lansing) annexed 1 square mile or more of township land; the seven cities' territorial growth totaled 11 square miles. Another 86 municipalities grew territorially between 0.1 and 1.0 square mile, totaling another 25 square miles collectively.[9]
- By contrast, Indiana's annexation laws function within a state with very soft townships that cannot resist municipal annexations. From 2000 to 2010, 63 municipalities (led by Fort Wayne) added 1 square mile or more of township land, totaling 300 square miles. Another 116 municipalities grew territorially between 0.1 and 1.0 square mile, totaling another 42 square miles collectively.[10]
- North Carolina has had arguably the country's most pro-annexation statutes. During the decade, 120 North Carolina municipalities each annexed more than 1.0 square mile, totaling 630 square miles of added territory, while another 166 annexed between 0.1 and 1.0 square mile, totaling another 68 square miles.[11]

In short, in the Age of Sprawl, Michigan's 532 cities and villages expanded their boundaries by only 1.9 percent during the past decade. By contrast, North Carolina's 542 cities, villages, and towns expanded their boundaries by 22.1 percent. But with a different set of rules of the game, in Michigan's neighboring state, Indiana's 567 municipalities expanded 16.6 percent—roughly comparable to the 22.1 percent expansion of North Carolina's municipalities and dwarfing fellow township state Michigan's 1.9 percent performance.

States should improve local annexation authority. For many small, relatively young metro areas, the central city's ability to annex urbanizing areas will be sufficient to maintain a basic unity of local government. Even in older, more built-up areas, opportunities often exist for annexation that would benefit central cities. Good municipal annexation laws as tools are important to improve a city's elasticity. Unfortunately, during the past two decades, the trend has been in the reverse direction. In many states (notably, in North Carolina, Tennessee, and Texas), state legislatures made annexation more difficult.[12]

Municipal annexation is authorized by general law in 44 states (Table 3.3). The exceptions are Hawaii and five of six New England states. However, Massachusetts's annexation laws (as well as those of New Jersey, New York, and Pennsylvania) grant only hypothetical powers because they were nullified by later statutes or by constitutional amendments.

Many states attach conditions that can severely inhibit a municipality's ability to annex. Thirty-four states allow the annexation process to be initiated by a petition of property owners in the area to be annexed. Usually the support of a majority or extraordinary majority of property owners is required. In nine of these states, annexation can be initiated *only* by property owner petition—a very severe limitation placing a city's expansion at the mercy of suburban developers and residents. By contrast, 32 states allow annexation to be initiated by city ordinance or resolution.

In 19 states, a referendum or majority approval of property owners in the area to be annexed is required—another tough hurdle except where large blocks of land are owned by a handful of proannexation developers. In 14 states, voters in the annexing city must approve the annexation—an invitation to opposition from nogrowth advocates or minority politicians fearing dilution of minority voting power.

In 11 states the affected county government must approve any municipal annexation. If the county fears loss of revenues or influence, this provision could be a very significant obstacle to municipal expansion.

How should the public good and private interests be balanced? I believe that state law should empower municipalities to initiate and carry out annexations while protecting property owners against unjust consequences. State statutes should protect annexed property

TABLE 3.3
STATE LAWS REGARDING MUNICIPAL ANNEXATIONS

	Number of states				
State law	South (16)	West (13)	Midwest (12)	Northeast (9)	U.S. total (50)
Municipal annexa- tion is authorized by state law	16	12	12	4	44
Annexation is initi- ated by property owner petition	12	10	9	3	34
Annexation is initiat- ed by city ordinance or resolution	12	9	10	1	32
Public hearing is required	10	8	7	2	27
Referendum and majority approval in city are required	8	2	4	0	14
Referendum or majority approval in area to be annexed is required	11	3	3	2	19
Approval of county governing authority is required	1	6	4	0	11

owners against increased taxes without commensurate increased services and against unwarranted intrusion in rural lifestyles, absent significant urbanization. However, the presumption should be that annexation will serve the larger public interest.

In general terms, a model state annexation statute would do the following:

- Set forth the standards by which an annexation would be deemed to serve the general public interest.
- Authorize annexation to be initiated either by petition by landowners or resolution by city council.

- Require public hearings and due process.
- Authorize annexation to be consummated by council action alone.
- Extend to affected landowners the right of appeal to the state's district court in the event landowners are aggrieved because the annexation was approved or rejected in violation of state standards.

LIMIT NEW MUNICIPALITIES

The ease or difficulty with which new municipalities are formed strongly affects the degree of fragmentation of urbanizing areas into multiple local governments. Virtually all states in the South, West, and Midwest set some limitations regarding minimum population, minimum area, or minimum tax base (Table 3.4). These limitations, however, tend to be modest. With the exception of New York, northeastern states are silent on the matter. In effect, the geopolitical maps of New England, New Jersey, New York, and Pennsylvania are set in concrete. (New York's law is an anachronism because new municipalities cannot be formed.)

Sixteen states require a minimum distance between the proposed and existing municipalities. (In New Mexico, for example, the distance is 5 miles.) This requirement is perhaps the most useful way to limit the formation of new municipalities.

Requirements regarding minimum population, minimum area, and minimum tax base should be set considerably higher than prevailing standards. State law also ought to provide for a substantial zone around existing municipalities in which the existing government can veto the incorporation of new municipalities or other public bodies, such as quasi-public water and sewer districts.

Finally, municipalities should be classified according to population size. Large cities should be given the presumptive authority over smaller cities to annex contested lands or even to absorb smaller cities in quasi-consolidation-type actions.[13] Small municipalities, in turn, should have the right to appeal such actions to state district court.

CREATE REGIONAL PARTNERSHIPS

A fourth state-based initiative is creating regional partnerships. Short of reshaping the local political map, states can authorize or mandate functional policies to achieve some of the benefits of metro

TABLE 3.4
STATE LAWS REGARDING FORMING NEW MUNICIPALITIES

State law	Number of states				
	South (16)	West (13)	Midwest (12)	Northeast (9)	U.S. total (50)
Limits are imposed on incorporation of new local government units	15	12	12	1	40
Minimum population is required	14	12	9	1	36
Minimum area is required	5	4	7	1	17
Minimum distance from existing units is required	8	3	5	0	16
Minimum ad valorem tax base is required	0	3	3	0	6

governments. Forty-two states specifically authorize local governments to enter into joint powers or joint service agreements. These agreements allow local governments to band together to address problems that transcend local political boundaries. For the most part, joint powers or joint service agreements address infrastructure issues (for example, sewage treatment and air quality management) or nonthreatening service needs (for example, emergency medical services and services for senior citizens). They rarely touch the core of social and economic divisions within metro areas—housing, schools, and fiscal disparities.

Creative exceptions exist, however. The Minnesota legislature mandated a multicounty tax-sharing compact for the Twin Cities area (revisit Box 3.3). In the Portland region, the Oregon legislature and area voters created a unique, independently elected metro government (revisit Box 3.2) both to administer several infrastructure services and, most important, to carry out regional land use and transportation planning. The state legislatures in Massachusetts,

Connecticut, and New Jersey directed suburban governments to participate in affordable housing programs.

A WORD ON COUNTY GOVERNMENT

Except in the Northeast and parts of the Midwest (revisit Box 3.5 on townships), counties have been the principal government of rural America. Counties predate urban development. They are the creation of a territorial or state legislature, which initially partitioned the territory or state's land into large governing units. As urbanization occurs, municipalities are formed to control development through planning and zoning and to provide a more intensive level of local services. Generally, county government continues to be responsible county-wide (including within municipalities) for certain services—county courts (state criminal trials), county assessor (property tax assessment), county treasurer (property tax collection), county clerk (records and elections), and often a county hospital (indigent health care). In addition, counties provide public services (typically, road and park maintenance and fire and police protection) to unincorporated areas.

County jurisdictions are remarkably stable. Today the United States has 3,033 counties; 50 years ago it had 3,052 counties.[14] Such stability gave rise to the adage that "the legislature may create municipalities, but only God can create a county."

Maryland is different, however, and I am a big fan of county government in Maryland. Even in highly urbanized areas, county government is usually the basic government. Baltimore County, for instance, covers 600 square miles, has 805,000 residents, and contains not a single municipality. (As an independent city separate and apart from Baltimore County, Baltimore City combines municipal and county functions.) With the nation's best mixed-income housing policies, growth management policies the equal of the Portland region's, and an outstanding county-wide school system, Montgomery County, in my judgment, is the country's best urban government. And thriving downtown Bethesda (with more restaurants than downtown Louisville or uptown Charlotte) and a resurgent downtown Silver Spring show that county government can "do cities" with the best of city governments.[15]

The most direct—and probably most efficient—path to creating metropolitan government in the majority of metro areas would be to empower urban county governments, have them absorb the functions and responsibilities of all municipal governments within their boundaries, and abolish all municipalities. This action is fully within the legal powers of most state legislatures even if at present such sweeping urban reorganization may be beyond legislators' desires and political powers.

However, absent such county-wide unification, empowering county governments to provide municipal-type services outside their city limits is the worst of all possible worlds for central cities. Such state action removes all incentives for suburban land developers or future suburban residents to support municipal annexation. County government as the vehicle for region-wide unification, yes! County government as just another competitor for central cities, no!

SUMMARIZING THE STATE REGIONAL REFORM AGENDA

We have now had four decades of experience with national models illustrating best practices in the three crucial areas for regional reforms:

- To diminish racial and economic segregation and eliminate concentrated poverty, Montgomery County, Maryland's inclusionary zoning law (see Box 3.1)
- To control suburban sprawl and reverse urban disinvestment, Oregon's tough Land Use Act, as implemented by Portland Metro (see Box 3.2)
- To reduce fiscal imbalances that result from uneven growth and socioeconomic imbalances, Minnesota's Fiscal Disparities Plan (see Box 3.3)

State governments should mandate these policies both for the myriad little boxes governments and for Big Box governments. Reformers should target governors and legislatures to adapt and adopt these successful changes in the rules of the game.

Woodrow Wilson called the states "the laboratory of democracy." America's urban problem presents states with their toughest challenge to live up to that billing.

Federal Government: Leveling the Playing Field

In any constitutional sense, the federal government has no role in the way in which local governments are organized within the states. Congress cannot, for example, mandate organization of metropolitan governments. Federal policy, nevertheless, has had a decisive impact on the emergence of suburban America since World War II and on the corresponding decline of many central cities:

- Since their inception, the Federal Housing Administration (1934) and the Veterans Administration (1944) have backed almost 60 million low-interest mortgages for single-family homes (largely in suburbia). By 2011, federal agencies insured or guaranteed mortgages for almost 9 million homeowners (about 20 percent of all mortgages; federal coverage peaked at 44 percent of all home mortgages in 1956). In addition, government-organized mortgage pools (Fannie Mae, Freddie Mac, and Ginnie Mae) held $5.4 *trillion* in mortgages in 2011.

- The Federal Highway Administration made automobile-based suburbs possible. From 1956 to 2011, the Federal Highway Administration spent about $1.4 trillion (in 2010 dollars) in federal aid for roads and highways (about two-thirds in urban areas). This figure was about five times the amount of federal aid for city-oriented mass transit ($282 billion in 2010 dollars).

- In 2011, the federal treasury did not collect over $77 billion in tax revenues because mortgage interest on homes (largely in the suburbs) is deductible. Another $24 billion a year in federal tax liability was waived as a credit for state and local property taxes paid. Added to that was over $18 billion a year as capital gains exclusions on home sales. In all, the federal government provided $119 billion in "tax expenditures" to subsidize largely suburban-oriented homeownership. By contrast, federal tax law currently provides only about $8 billion a year in Low-Income Housing Tax Credits to subsidize largely city-oriented rental housing, and U.S. Department of Housing and Urban Development housing assistance programs for low-income households total about $40 billion annually.

Even in an era of shrinking federal aid to state and local government, federal policy continues to promote urban sprawl and the resultant decline of inelastic central cities. For 60 years "national urban policy" has been a "national *suburban* policy."

If, as I believe, the "action" is really with state and local governments—and with citizens as state and local voters—what can the federal government do to encourage forming metropolitan governments? More to the point, how can the federal government reform its own policies and practices to give inelastic central cities and their

poor minority residents, if not preferential advantages, then at least
an even break?

FEDERAL POLICY: BACK TO THE FUTURE?

When I first wrote *Cities without Suburbs* in 1992, our national debt
had more than quadrupled to $4.4 trillion during the 12 years of the
Ronald Reagan and George H. W. Bush administrations. Experts
forecast a long-term Social Security crisis as baby boomers aged, but
Washington chose to focus on short-term problems.

When the book's second edition appeared in 1995, the Bill Clinton
administration's 1993 tax increase and several years of budget dis-
cipline had just begun to shrink the annual federal deficit. By fiscal
year 1998, with federal revenues soaring as a result of the booming economy, the federal budget embarked on a four-year period
of budget surpluses that would actually allow paying down the national debt (at least, the so-called publicly held portion).[16] Prosperity allowed the president and Congress to project more time before
the Social Security crunch would arrive.

As I wrote *Cities without Suburbs: A Census 2000 Update*, with the
economy in recession, a war on terrorism to fight, and George W.
Bush's $1.3 trillion tax cut eroding federal revenues, a projected sur-
plus had been converted into red ink as far as disinterested econo-
mists could project. The Social Security crisis came 10 years closer
(as well as the arrival of my own retirement years) but was now
eclipsed by the runaway growth of Medicare costs.

This edition of *Cities without Suburbs* comes as the country strug-
gles to recover from the financial sector meltdown—caused Great
Recession of 2008. On Inauguration Day 2009, President Barack
Obama inherited a $10.6 trillion national debt—78 percent of which
had been run up under self-proclaimed fiscally conservative Republican presidents named Reagan and Bush.

To counteract the most severe economic crisis since the Great Depression of the 1930s, the federal government incurred $1 trillion
annual deficits to pump up the economy. As this edition goes to
press, our national debt has risen to $16.5 trillion with more years of
red ink still projected.

"Incentives" is a euphemism for federal money—either dollars
spent or taxes not paid. Placing most central city governments on
a sound financial basis, reducing regional racial and economic segregation, slowing urban sprawl—these are outcomes for which it
would be worth considering federal incentives.

In the first edition of *Cities without Suburbs,* I proposed a series of incentives from the federal government that would reward local citizens and communities for forming metro governments. I proposed increasing the federal income tax deduction allowed for local taxes paid to metro governments, boosting the tax credit allowed for purchasing bonds issued by metro governments, and adding bonuses to grant-in-aid allocations (except Medicaid) received by metro governments.

Two decades later, the federal government politically cannot afford to put major new money on the table for any domestic purpose except putting Social Security and Medicare on a sound footing and shrinking the federal deficit. So let me suggest how six decades of federal suburban policy can be changed to slow urban sprawl and reverse the trend toward greater economic segregation (particularly of inner-city Blacks and Hispanics) *without* spending more money. (For the facts about whether we could afford to raise taxes and spend more on building a healthier nation, see Box 3.8.)

SLOWING URBAN SPRAWL

Federal grant-in-aid programs for large public works pay a big portion of the bill for urban sprawl. Federal highway funds ($43.2 billion in fiscal year 2012) and water system and sewage treatment grants ($5.3 billion in fiscal year 2012) have had the greatest impact. With the federal share varying from 75 percent to 90 percent, financing major sprawl-oriented infrastructure has been virtually free for state and local governments. Let's talk about modifying how the federal government should subsidize future infrastructure projects.

Congress has already put in place regional transportation planning (see Box 3.9). Congress should now put anti-sprawl teeth into that system. It should require metropolitan planning organizations (MPOs) to analyze the impact of each project on the metropolitan area's residential density (using densities from the Census 2010 as the baseline). A sliding scale for federal participation would be established for each grant-in-aid program. For example, if a proposed widening of an urban-aid highway reaching out to the metropolitan periphery would promote more sprawl and new residential development at densities 50 percent below the region's average residential density, federal participation would be reduced from 75 percent of total project costs to 25 percent. Conversely, for building a light-rail line that would encourage new development at 25 percent above the region's average residential density, federal participation would increase from 75 percent to 90 percent.

Box 3.8 Americans' Taxes Are Too High?
Compared to Whose?

For 30 years, the conservative mantra has been "Americans are overtaxed ... Americans are overtaxed." Well, compared to whom?

Every year the Organisation for Economic Co-operation and Development (OECD)[a] totals up national, state, and local government taxes of all types and compares the total to the gross domestic product (GDP) of each of its 34 member nations. Consider this the effective tax rate for each country. (See box table.)

As a factual matter, the United States has the *third-lowest tax rate* among the 34 OECD members and has been third or fourth lowest for at least a decade.

The Heritage Foundation[b] has used the same methodology to calculate effective tax rates for 178 counties as part of the Fiscal Freedom section of its Index of Economic Freedom. For 2007, the Heritage Foundation calculated the U.S. tax rate as a share of GDP as 28.2 percent (the same as the OECD calculation for that year). The United States ranked 131st lowest of 178 that year.

Discounting oil-exporting countries (whose oil wealth and relatively small populations minimize tax collections), one finds that topping the Heritage Foundation's fiscal freedom rankings in 2007 were Chad, Burma (Myanmar), the Republic of the Congo, Afghanistan, and Yemen (with effective tax rates ranging from 4.2 percent to 7.1 percent). At the bottom of the fiscal freedom rankings in 2007 were France (46.1 percent), Belgium (46.8 percent), Sweden (49.7 percent), Denmark (50.0 percent), and three anomalies (whose statistics are probably more than unusually unreliable): Zimbabwe (49.3 percent), Kiribati (Gilbert Islands) (91.6 percent), and Timor-Leste (East Timor)(109.7 percent).

Taxes are the dues we pay for the privilege of living in a civilized community.

Using the MPO structure, Congress should require regional planning for other federal infrastructure grants-in-aid. Oregon congressman Earl Blumenauer (a former Portland city commissioner) advocates creating a "water ISTEA" covering federal water and sewer system grants.

The underlying principle is simple: if state and local governments want more urban sprawl, they should finance the lion's share of the costs themselves through increased state and local taxes and users fees.

Total Revenue as a Percentage of GDP in 2010		
Rank order	*Country*	*Effective tax rate (%)*
1	Denmark	48.2
2	Sweden	45.8
3	Belgium	43.8
4	Italy	43.0
5	France	42.9
13	Germany	36.3
15	United Kingdom	35.0
	OECD average (34 countries)	33.9
21	New Zealand	31.3
23	Canada	31.0
28	Japan	26.9
30	Australia	25.9
31	South Korea	25.1
32	**United States**	**24.8**
33	Chile	20.9
34	Mexico	18.1

a. Founded in 1961, the mission of the Paris-based OECD is "to promote policies that will improve the economic and social well-being of people around the world" (http://www.oecd.org).

b. Founded in 1973, the Washington, D.C.–based Heritage Foundation "is a research and educational institution—a think tank—whose mission is to formulate and promote conservative public policies based on the principles of free enterprise, limited government, individual freedom, traditional American values, and a strong national defense" (http://www.heritage.org).

REVERSING ECONOMIC SEGREGATION

In 1990, 2,726 high-poverty census tracts where poverty rates exceeded 40 percent existed in the nation's metropolitan areas. Most had federal public housing projects located in or adjacent to them. Nothing in the private housing market had produced as much concentrated poverty as federal public housing policy.

Box 3.9 "Ice Tea": The Fed's Regional Brew

After languishing at the federal level throughout the 1980s, regionalism was revived in 1991 when Congress passed the Intermodal Surface Transportation Efficiency Act (ISTEA). The initiative was further strengthened with the law's reenactment in 1998 as the Transportation Equity Act for the 21st Century (TEA-21) and, subsequently, in 2005 as the Safe, Accountable, Flexible, Efficient Transportation Equity Act: A Legacy for Users (SAFETEA-LU). (Congress abandoned its acronymic penchant with the two-year extension of the law as the Federal Public Transportation Act of 2012.)

Since 1973, local governments have been involved in planning the use of certain federal funds for transportation. ISTEA authorized $151 billion over six years (fiscal years 1992–97) for highway and transit assistance, TEA-21 followed with $222 billion for six years (FY 1998–2003), and SAFETEA-LU continued funding with $286 billion for another six years (FY 2004–09).[a]

The key change was the greater discretion afforded local officials in the use of federal funds. In past decades, local planning was largely limited to prioritizing laundry lists of projects within narrow, federally prescribed program allocations. Under ISTEA, TEA-21, and SAFETEA-LU, MPOs for all urbanized areas with 200,000 or more residents have broad discretion to allocate lump-sum federal funds among road, bridge, and transit projects.

About half of all MPOs are "regional councils," voluntary consortia of local governments with a variety of program interests be-

---

In the first edition of *Cities without Suburbs*, I added my voice to the many that were calling for radical overhaul of the federal public housing program. "Housing the urban poor in high-density, inner-city public housing projects is patently destructive and should be ended as soon as possible," I wrote. "The federal court–ordered Gautreaux Project in the Chicago area has demonstrated the striking effectiveness of metrowide [rent subsidies].... The federal government should adopt a Gautreaux-type strategy for public housing on a nationwide scale." (See Box 3.10.)

By the turn of the millennium, a total restructuring of federal public housing policy was well under way. The Department of Housing and Urban Development was tearing down more than 100,000 high-density, often high-rise projects and replacing them with low-density townhouses and garden apartments. Most important, these

yond transportation planning. Other MPOs are regional economic development organizations, transportation planning agencies, and arms of state highway departments.

In the judgment of the National Association of Regional Councils, ISTEA and TEA-21 "mark[ed] a radical and visionary transformation in the nation's transportation policy."[b]

But it is more than just about roads and rail lines. Transportation networks shape how and where people live, work, and play. Until ISTEA, TEA-21, and SAFETEA-LU, the Federal Highway Administration and state highway departments were the masters of—not the servants of—regional land use planning.

Only the Portland and Minneapolis–St. Paul regions have regional governments combining real land use and transportation planning powers. Some regions, such as Seattle–King County, have large county governments that exercise such authority. But for most metropolitan areas, multigovernment designated MPOs are the only bodies where grassroots movements can lobby for regional reforms.

a. Since that time, fierce partisan and ideological splits have prevented congressional agreement on a long-term reauthorization, resulting in 11 short-term extensions through March 2012 and a two-year extension shortly thereafter.

b. National Association of Regional Councils, *Regional Reporter* 3 (January 1992): 1.

were mixed-income communities with as few as 25 percent of the residents being very-low-income families. In addition, the federal Section 8 (housing choice voucher) program had expanded to subsidize rents for 2.2 million very-low-income families (greatly exceeding the number of project-based apartments).

However, inner-city slums, anchored by large public housing projects, must not simply be replaced by suburban slums, filled with poor households using their vouchers to rent hand-me-down houses or cheap private apartments built for the voucher market. The goal is to assimilate low-income households into standard housing in predominantly middle-class communities. Therefore, federal regulations are essential to prevent too many poor households from reconcentrating in older suburban areas. For example, federal regulations should not allow vouchers to exceed one-third

---

Box 3.10 From Failure in the Ghetto
to Success in the Suburbs

The Gautreaux Project proved that public housing tenants in inner cities can succeed simply by getting out of bad neighborhoods into better neighborhoods. The project was named for public housing tenant activist Dorothy Gautreaux, lead plaintiff in a suit brought in 1976 in which the federal courts found the Chicago Housing Authority (CHA) guilty of racial discrimination. One remedy the courts ordered was to subsidize moving public housing families out of CHA projects and into private rental housing elsewhere in Chicago or anywhere in Chicago's six-county suburban area.

Between 1981 and 1998 more than 7,100 families participated in the program, administered by the Leadership Council for Metropolitan Open Communities, a court-appointed nonprofit organization. One-third of the families remained in Chicago; two-thirds moved to Chicago's suburbs.

James E. Rosenbaum, professor of sociology at Northwestern University, did a follow-up study of the "city stayers" and "suburban movers."[a] Both showed the same socioeconomic profile entering the program: typically a Black female head of household who was receiving welfare assistance and had two or three children. Of the suburban-mover mothers, 64 percent were working, compared with 51 percent for city-stayer mothers. Of the suburban-mover children, 95 percent graduated from their suburban systems, compared with a graduation rate of 80 percent of city stayers from Chicago schools. Fifty-four percent of suburban movers had continued their education (27 percent in four-year colleges), compared with

---

of all rental units in an apartment building or might limit vouchers to neighborhoods where the poverty rate is less than 150 percent of the area's poverty rate. (If the metro poverty rate were 10 percent, vouchers could not be used in census tracts with poverty rates of more than 15 percent.)

Does sufficient affordable housing exist in suburban areas to assimilate poor families from inner-city housing markets? Certainly a substantial amount exists; after all, most poor Whites live in suburban neighborhoods. A few communities have voluntarily mandated mixed-income housing development, such as Montgomery County, Maryland (revisit Box 3.1).

Here again, a shift in federal policy can help. After decades of fostering redlining of inner-city neighborhoods, the federal govern-

21 percent of city stayers (4 percent in four-year colleges). Seventy-five percent of suburban-mover youth were working (21 percent for hourly wages of $6.50 or better); by contrast, only 41 percent of city-stayer youth had a job (5 percent at $6.50 or better per hour).[b]

"Pessimistic predictions of 'culture of poverty' models are not supported," Rosenbaum concluded after completing his study. "The early experiences of low-income blacks do not prevent them from benefiting from suburban moves."[c]

One participant in the Gautreaux Project summed up her experience: "[A housing project] deteriorates you. You don't want to do anything. [Living in the suburbs] made me feel that I'm worth something. I can do anything I want to do if I get up and try it."[d]

The Gautreaux Project had a major impact on federal housing assistance policies, turning HUD away from concentrating poor families in large projects toward integrating them in mixed-income communities through rent vouchers used on a region-wide basis and tearing down large projects and rebuilding them as mixed-income neighborhoods under HOPE VI grants.

a. James E. Rosenbaum, "Black Pioneers—Do Their Moves to the Suburbs Increase Economic Opportunity for Mothers and Children?" *Housing Policy Debate* 2, no.4 (1991): 1179–213.

b. Outcomes for both suburban movers and city stayers were presumably superior to those for households remaining in many of Chicago's high-rise public housing projects.

c. Rosenbaum, "Black Pioneers," 1203.

d. Ibid., 1192.

ment is redirecting private mortgage funds toward inner-city areas. The Community Reinvestment Act (CRA) requires mortgage lenders to meet new targets for mortgage and renovation loans in older neighborhoods. The federally chartered secondary mortgage market agencies such as Fannie Mae and Freddie Mac must ensure that 20 percent of lending they back occurs in central cities.[17]

Overall, such requirements have helped level the playing field. Ironically, however, sometimes meeting CRA goals has resulted in mortgage lenders helping build low-income housing projects precisely where they should not be built: in already poverty-impacted inner-city neighborhoods. The CRA and other federal regulations should be amended to allow mixed-income housing, accessible to former public housing tenants, in suburban areas to meet federal goals as well.

Box 3.11 Partnership for Sustainable Communities

A most promising initiative to change the rules of the game at the federal level was launched in June 2009, when Shaun Donovan, secretary of the U.S. Department of Housing and Urban Development; Ray LaHood, secretary of the U.S. Department of Transportation; and Lisa Jackson, administrator of the U.S. Environmental Protection Agency announced that the three agencies had formed a Partnership for Sustainable Communities.

The overall goal of the partnership is "to help American families in all communities—rural, suburban, and urban—gain better access to affordable housing, more transportation options, and lower transportation costs." The three agencies pledged "to work together to ensure that these housing and transportation goals are met while simultaneously protecting the environment, promoting equitable development, and helping to address the challenges of climate change."[a]

The partnership's first undertaking was the Sustainable Communities Initiative (SCI), for which Congress appropriated $150 million in fiscal year 2010 and $100 million in fiscal year 2011.

On behalf of Building ONE America (see Box 4.1), I provided 10 detailed recommendations to the three agencies regarding the regulations that they should adopt to shape the SCI program for maximum impact.[b]

Assessing the final regulations several months later, Building ONE America praised the fact that the SCI planning grant program would be truly regional in scope and had placed achieving regional equity goals on a par with environmental protection goals.

Moreover, Fannie Mae and Freddie Mac sponsor many special mortgage programs to achieve different social goals, such as encouraging more minority homeownership or helping first-time buyers. They should adopt a new policy to reward communities for implementing inclusionary zoning policies. All homeowners in an inclusionary neighborhood should be eligible for lower-interest loans (say, one point below prevailing market). To qualify, an inclusionary neighborhood would have to meet two tests: (a) having at least 15 or 20 percent affordable housing and (b) having a regional public housing agency acquire one-third of the affordable units.

The greatest fear (at least, expressed fear) of homeowners to the mixed-income concept is that having lower-income neighbors would reduce the value of their market-rate homes. In the context

However, the bar had been set too low for prospective SCI grant-ees. The federal agencies would not be requiring grantees to do rigorous regional opportunity mapping and then shape their proposals to overcome the great disparities revealed in their "geography of opportunity." In particular, Building ONE America urged that the federal regulations require that all housing developed in conjunction with SCI grants be mixed-income housing and be supported by regional housing mobility counseling and placement programs.

With the $250 million over two fiscal years, SCI provided planning and implementation grants to 134 communities, with MPOs at the heart of many of the multiagency, multigovernmental coalitions created to carry out their programs.

Ultimately, the key to the Partnership for Sustainable Communities will be not how effectively $250 million in SCI grants will be used but how lessons learned in creating sustainable, inclusive communities will be applied to the $145 billion in grants-in-aid to state and local governments that the three agencies make annually.

a. Quotations are from the initial press release, Partnership for Sustainable Communities, http://www.sustainablecommunities.gov/aboutUs.html.

b. David Rusk, "Building Sustainable, Inclusive Communities: How America Can Pursue Smart Growth and Reunite Our Metropolitan Communities," Poverty and Race Research Action Council, Washington, DC, http://www.prrac.org/pdf/SustainableInclusiveCommunities.pdf.

of a Montgomery County–type policy, that fear is ungrounded (revisit Box 3.1). However, providing lower-interest mortgages to all homeowners would convert that economic fear into an undeniable economic benefit in the form of lower mortgage payments for everyone in the neighborhood.

This proposed federal regional reform agenda is based on two principles. First, it echoes the old Hippocratic oath: "Do no more harm." Second, it reflects the ups and downs of the federal fiscal and budgetary teeter-totter: "Spend no more money." If the federal government truly reformed the way it did business in urban America as outlined above, state and local governments *might* be motivated to change substantially the way they approached metropolitan development issues—that is, the rules of the game (see Box 3.11).

Box 3.12 Organizing Grassroots
and Grass-Tops Wins Big Victory in New Jersey

In June 2008, the New Jersey legislature approved the Housing Reform Act of 2008, the most important state housing legislation in the nation over the past two decades.

The legislative victory culminated a five-year campaign by the New Jersey Regional Coalition that, in turn, built on the long battle waged by Peter O'Connor and the Fair Share Housing Center over the previous three decades.[a]

The journey began with a lawsuit—*Southern Burlington County NAACP v. Mt. Laurel Township*—brought by O'Connor in 1971. In 1975, the New Jersey Supreme Court rendered its epochal *Mt. Laurel* decision, ruling that each of New Jersey's 566 municipalities has a constitutional obligation to provide for a "fair share" of affordable housing—a fair share determined not just by the demographics within the boundaries of each municipality but based on the multimunicipal regional need.

For a decade, the New Jersey legislature ignored the court's call to adopt implementing legislation. It then enacted the Fair Housing Act of 1985, which, in effect, worked to water down the court's ruling as much as possible.

The biggest escape clause was the provision regarding so-called Regional Contribution Agreements (RCAs), by which wealthy suburbs would bribe poor cities and boroughs to take over up to half of their fair-share affordable housing obligation. Over the next 20 years, wealthy suburbs paid out $210 million to escape their constitutional obligation to build 10,256 units of affordable housing in their own communities.

In June 2003, the newly organized New Jersey Regional Coalition (NJRC) targeted repealing RCAs, labeling them "blood money." Among knowledgeable politicos, the universal view was that RCAs could never be repealed: RCAs were too popular with both wealthy "sending" suburbs and mayors of poor "receiving" cities and boroughs, whose financially stressed communities were desperate for any source of additional revenues.

However, the NJRC offered the following documentation:

- RCAs slammed the doors shut to high-opportunity towns with their rapidly growing job supply; low-poverty, high-performance schools; and high-quality municipal services.
- At the same time, RCAs cemented thousands of poor children into places with vanishing jobs; high-poverty, low-performance schools; and poor-quality municipal services.[b]
- Furthermore, shutting the door to high-opportunity, growing outer suburbs increased pressures on older inner suburbs with their more affordable housing supply.

In key legislative districts throughout the state, the NJRC brought 200 to 300 grassroots constituents demanding RCA repeal to confront their legislators. The coalition organized the "grass-tops" — First Suburbs mayors—to speak out publicly for RCA repeal and to counter the pro-RCA lobbying of the state League of Municipalities, which supposedly represented all 566 municipalities but consistently supported the wealthiest members' interests. The NJRC convinced every bishop to condemn RCAs as "immoral" and every major daily newspaper to call for RCA repeal.

Most important, the NJRC helped recruit Joe Roberts, Speaker of the Assembly, to be primary sponsor and champion of RCA repeal. Roberts's Housing Reform Act of 2008 contained sweeping provisions, including eliminating RCAs; requiring a 20 percent set-aside for affordable housing in all state-aided housing developments; directing that federal Low-Income Housing Tax Credits be used in mixed-income, market-rate developments in low-poverty, high-opportunity towns; requiring at least 25 percent of all affordable housing be targeted to extremely low-poverty families (less than 30 percent of area median income); requiring towns to spend municipal housing trust fund dollars on affordable housing within their borders; and mandating that municipalities provide density bonuses to developers constructing inclusionary housing.

After weeks of tough battling in the 2008 session, on June 16, by a vote of 45 to 33 in the Assembly and, on June 23, by a vote of 21 to 16 in the Senate, the New Jersey legislature repealed the "odious and exploitative"[c] RCAs and enacted the bill's other provisions.

Thirty-three years after the court's decision, 23 years after the legislature created the giant RCA loophole, and 5 years after the NJRC began its campaign to repeal RCAs, the state of New Jersey had finally been brought to adopt housing and school policies to achieve the vision of the historic *Mt. Laurel* suit: an economically and racially integrated society.

a. For a more thorough account of the legislative campaign, see David Rusk, "The 'Outside Game': Can Faith Move Mountain-less New Jersey?" in *Breakthrough Communities: Sustainability and Justice in the Next American Metropolis*, ed. M. Paloma Pavel (Cambridge, MA: MIT Press, 2009), 265–83.

b. In testimony before the legislature, the NJRC showed that the 149 RCA senders gained more than 124,000 jobs while the 50 RCA receivers lost more than 12,000 jobs during the 1990s, RCAs' most active years; that only 4 percent of the children in the 149 RCA senders were low income, compared with 44 percent in the 50 RCA receivers (a sure indicator of academic performance levels; see Box 2.5); and that the 149 RCA senders had three times the tax base per capita ($133,161) of the 50 RCA receivers ($45,989) in 2001 (a measure of relative ability to provide municipal services).

c. This language was used by Speaker of the Assembly Roberts in a speech at Princeton University in 2004.

BUILDING GRASSROOTS COALITIONS

What *will* motivate state and local governments to change their ways are politically powerful grassroots reform movements. As I stated in the preface, "what these two decades have taught me most is that building political coalitions to achieve fundamental reforms in the rules of the game is hard, time-consuming work."

Over the past two decades, I have worked with many different individuals and organizations in more than 120 metropolitan areas: affordable housing advocates, civil rights organizations, environmental groups and farmland preservation advocates,[18] university-based urban studies centers, MPOs, state municipal leagues and associations of counties, chambers of commerce and business leadership organizations, and philanthropic foundations.

Many have made important contributions and have undertaken good faith efforts to secure regional reforms. All, however, have usually lacked one key dimension: the ability to mobilize large numbers of people.

In a June 2010 Gallup poll, 43 percent of Americans report that they attend their church, synagogue, or mosque regularly ("at least once a week" or "almost every week"). Quite simply, as the civil rights movement demonstrated, faith communities can be the fulcrum for organizing popular reform movements.

For 15 years, I worked with a network of faith-based coalitions committed to changing the rules of the game through metropolitan- and state-level action. Affiliated with the Chicago-based Gamaliel Foundation, congregations organized across denominational lines; across racial, ethnic, and class divides; and across city, borough or village, and town or township boundaries for political action. Their targets were city halls and county courthouses (in Big Box states) and state capitols (in little boxes states). The most effective of these coalitions scored some spectacular victories (revisit Box 3.12).

But I also learned that such reform campaigns must be carefully targeted to those communities that share common self-interests and must be shaped to weave together workable majorities in city councils, county commissions, state legislatures, and (with the advent of the Obama administration) the halls of Congress.

Organizing just city constituencies is a losing proposition. In 2000, central cities collectively represented only 26 percent of their states' populations (hence, 26 percent of voting strength in their legislatures, if that).[19]

The key battleground is the First Suburbs—the older, inner, suburban communities developed before or shortly after World War II. They are frequently the first- and second-ring towns and school districts outside big cities and industrial centers.

These communities, once known for their exclusivity and even restrictive practices, are increasingly diverse and today are the most reflective of our nation's changing demographics. They are rapidly becoming our nation's real melting pot as they continue to be destinations for families from all walks of life seeking opportunity, diversity, safe neighborhoods, good schools, and high-quality municipal services.

But these First Suburbs are now experiencing "city problems": surging poverty, struggling schools, aging infrastructure, declining revenue, and rising tax rates are beginning to overwhelm more and more of these communities and their local leaders.

They are often overlooked by federal and state policy makers and passed over by many regional, urban, and community development programs. Moreover, federal and state policies and investments have often reinforced or contributed to the regional disparities that have put many older suburbs and our most diverse communities at risk.

Yet any regional opportunity assessment would show First Suburbs representing 40 percent to 60 percent of the region's population. A First Suburb–central city alliance would command two-thirds or more of the voting power in most state legislatures and, potentially, the Congress.

Organizing the First Suburbs in key areas of the country is the mission of Building ONE America, as discussed in the next chapter in Box 4.1.

Notes

1. I am indebted to Dr. John P. Blair of Wright State University for coining the phrase "elasticity mimics."

2. The wave of school district consolidations took place in the late-1950s and 1960s amid concern about creating more comprehensive high schools to improve America's competitiveness during the Cold War. Generating great controversy, school consolidations (particularly in rural areas) were the work of state legislatures directly or by state boards of education as empowered by their legislatures. Few legislators who supported school consolidations were subsequently reelected—a lesson not lost on 21st-century legislators.

3. The 11 independent cities are Washington, D.C.; Baltimore; St. Louis; and 8 larger cities in Virginia. In all, Virginia has 40 independent cities, ranging in size from Virginia Beach (437,994) to Norton (3,958).

4. The 14 surrounded cities are Los Angeles, Oakland, Miami, Atlanta, Chicago, Detroit, Grand Rapids, Minneapolis, Cincinnati, Cleveland, Dayton, Toledo, Dallas, and Milwaukee.

5. Group 2 states are Alabama, Arizona, Arkansas, Delaware, Idaho, Iowa, Maryland, Mississippi, Missouri, Nebraska, North Dakota, Oklahoma, South Dakota, Texas, West Virginia, and Wyoming. All have weak townships or are county states.

6. Group 3 states are California, Colorado, Nevada, New Mexico, North Carolina, Oregon, South Carolina, Utah, and Washington, as well as Alaska, Florida, Georgia, Indiana, Kansas, Kentucky, Louisiana, Montana, and Tennessee, where postwar consolidations have occurred. All are county states except Indiana, whose townships are very weak.

7. In Virginia, technically a half-dozen city–county consolidations occurred, such as Virginia Beach–Princess Anne County in the Hampton Roads area. However, all were really maneuvers to municipalize suburban counties to prevent further annexations by Norfolk, Portsmouth, and Newport News.

8. Central cities that could not annex land included 95 in New England, New York, New Jersey, and Pennsylvania; Virginia's 15 larger independent cities; and about two dozen older central cities (such as Cleveland, Detroit, and Chicago) that were completed surrounded by incorporated suburbs or were already consolidated city–counties (such as Baltimore, Denver, New Orleans, Philadelphia, San Francisco, and St. Louis, as well as the more recent consolidations mentioned).

9. Between 2000 and 2010, another 212 Michigan municipalities were shown as increasing their municipal area by less than 0.1 of a square mile (i.e., less than 64 acres), and 226 municipalities are shown as losing tiny amounts of municipal territory. Because formal detachments of municipal land are extremely rare, I have assumed that the apparent loss of municipal territory represents the result of more accurate, satellite-based surveying, particularly in the calculation of the deduction for acreage involved in rivers, creeks, and lakes. Similarly, I have assumed that any apparent addition of new territory of less than 64 acres also represents more precise surveying without denying the possibility of small, voluntary annexations or the outcome of riverfront and lakefront reclamation.

10. To complete the picture, 258 Indiana municipalities "grew" by less than 0.1 square mile and another 130 municipalities experienced tiny apparent losses.

11. To complete the picture, 150 North Carolina municipalities grew by less than 0.1 square mile, and another 105 municipalities experienced tiny apparent losses.

12. Anti-annexation movements are often led by newcomers in these states who have moved from little boxes states. (In the 2000s, 40 percent of newcomers to North Carolina came from little boxes states.) Whether the issue is annexation or student assignment plans in county-wide school districts, the newcomers'

argument is, "Well, that's not the way we did it back in New York (or Pennsylvania or Michigan or wherever)." Such newcomers never acknowledge that, in terms of ending the "segregation of opportunity," it didn't work well in New York or wherever. Of course, re-creating Northern-style exclusive enclaves just for themselves is often such reformers' goal.

13. Nebraska is the only state that authorizes a larger municipality to annex a smaller municipality (defined as fewer than 10,000 residents). In the early 2000s, the small city of Elkhorn (7,779 residents in 2000) bid to annex a large swath of territory lying to the west of Omaha (399,357 residents), which, if successful, would cut off Omaha's last remaining growth path, rendering it an inelastic city. In response, Omaha initiated action not only to annex the contested land but also to annex the city of Elkhorn. In January 2007, the Nebraska Supreme Court ruled that Elkhorn technically "ceased to exist" when Omaha's annexation ordinance took effect in March 2005.

14. The Census Bureau tabulates consolidated city–counties as municipalities, a procedure that accounts for the net reduction in the number of counties.

15. Both Bethesda and Silver Spring are simply unincorporated census-designated places without any municipal governments. Montgomery County government is their local general government.

16. Since fiscal year 1966, the federal government's practice has been to record payroll taxes for Social Security as general revenue rather than as an earmarked trust fund (like gasoline taxes). In its place, the federal government simply records an IOU within the Social Security accounts. Thus, as of February 6, 2013, the national debt of $16,479,954,658,103.57 was divided into two parts: $11,625,346,979,571.39 as "debt held by the public" (the "public" being, for example, you, your pension plan, your college's endowment fund, and the Chinese) and $4,854,607,678,532.18 as "intragovernmental holdings" (a euphemism for the IOU in the Social Security accounts). These data can be accessed at http://www.publicdebt.treas.gov/.

17. In July 2008, in the midst of the financial market meltdown, the federal government took over Fannie Mae and Freddie Mac, firing their management and boards of directors, and placing them under the conservatorship of the Federal Housing Finance Agency.

18. Jack Laurie, president of the Michigan Farm Bureau, memorably stated, "To save our farms, we must save our cities."

19. Ironically, in 2000, the only state where designated central cities were a majority of the state's population (53 percent) was Arizona, based on the designation of wealthy Scottsdale as a central city. With the massive population of New York City, New York came close (49 percent); indeed, the New York City delegation generally controls the Assembly (the lower house). With its multiple, highly elastic central cities, Texas also came close (46 percent), though in such a conservative state many "city" legislators do not champion progressive legislation. By contrast, in little boxes states such as Pennsylvania, central cities totaled only 22 percent of the state's population; in Michigan, only 21 percent; and in New Jersey, only 11 percent.

Chapter 4

Conclusion

"You may have shifted from a theme of cities without suburbs to suburbs with incidental cities," commented my colleague Hank Savitch in 1992 after reviewing an early draft of the first edition of this book.

"Your central argument," Hank continued, "is that cities 'succeed' only if they continue to absorb suburbs, which you see as America's preferred lifestyle. City survival ought not be so dependent upon imitating suburban patterns. How can cities become viable again within a metropolitan environment? Frankly, I believe that cities do have different roles to play."

His comments brought me up short. I love old-fashioned, bustling downtowns, and I love the old apartment buildings and townhouses, nearby shops, tree-lined streets, mini-parks, buses, and subways of good urban neighborhoods. Nothing is sadder than a city that undertakes a redevelopment project that looks and functions like a suburban office park and shopping mall.

As mayor, I often spoke of Albuquerque as "a giant suburb in search of a city." Albuquerque had all the suburban lifestyle its advocates could possibly want, I suggested. Albuquerque needed to strengthen its urban character. With modest success and much controversy, I promoted downtown Albuquerque as a center of business, government, entertainment, and the arts.

Having returned to Washington, D.C., in 1991, my wife, Delcia, and I live again in the District of Columbia in a condominium 12 minutes from the White House. At our front door is a Metro bus stop; at our back door, a 2-mile-long ribbon of wooded trails. Two food markets, two pharmacies, barbershops and beauty salons, three dry cleaners, a florist, two banks, two liquor stores, seven restaurants, two Starbucks, and a dozen other stores lie within a 10-minute walk.

The choice that Delcia and I made to live in the city when we returned to the Washington area was not unusual. During the past two decades, tens of thousands of empty nesters like us moved back to many cities around the country. The demographic impact of returning empty nesters was certainly exceeded by the hundreds of thousands of young professionals—singles, "mingles," young marrieds without children, gay couples—who opted for the diversity, excitement, cultural richness, and convenience of big-city living. The core areas of Washington, Baltimore, Cleveland, Philadelphia, Portland, and several dozen more older cities began to thrive with an urban vitality that in previous decades seemed to have been preserved only by New York, Chicago, Boston, Seattle, and San Francisco. Many downtowns and surrounding historic neighborhoods, beefed up with new condominiums and townhouses, became virtual "yuppie theme parks." Certainly, this was one of the "different roles" that cities could play that Hank Savitch alluded to.

Another different role was a traditional function that many cities recovered in recent decades as the doorway to a new life for millions of immigrants. A cherished chapter of our national legend (at least, in retrospect) is how millions of European immigrants—Germans, Irish, Italians, Greeks, Poles, and other Eastern Europeans—first touched our shores at Ellis Island and then fanned out into their new country's cities to staff the factories of the world's emerging industrial power.

That historic flow of immigrants was largely suspended from the early 1920s through the mid-1960s, in part because of the Great Depression, World War II, the Cold War, and thereafter, Europe's economic revival. Most important, however, Congress enacted a very restrictive immigration law in 1924 that established quotas based on the national origins of the American population as of the 1890 census. This law effectively slammed the door in the face of most would-be immigrants who were from Asia, Latin America, and Africa. (Fifteen million African Americans, whose ancestors were brought to America as slaves, were not accorded the dignity of a "national origin.") Only in 1965 did Congress liberalize America's immigration laws again.

Thus, for the first two postwar decades, many older cities (which were often inelastic cities as well) were confronted by three simultaneous demographic trends: White middle-class families moving to the burgeoning new suburbs, rural Blacks moving from southern farms into cities south and north, and a relative trickle of immigrants arriving from abroad. For inelastic central cities, it was a formula for steady decline in total population combined with rapid increase in the proportion of African Americans.

During the 1990s, however, swelling immigration lifted the United States to its highest rate of population growth since the postwar baby boom. Though immigration slowed with the Great Recession, Census 2010 recorded the highest percentage of foreign-born residents (12.6 percent) since 1910. Massive immigration reversed the population decline of some inelastic cities. For example, of the 137 principal central cities studied in Chapter 2, 30 were inelastic cities that could not (or did not) annex new land but still saw population increases during recent decades. Hispanic immigration accounted totally for the net population increases in 21 of the 30 cities.[1] Hispanic and Asian immigration combined accounted completely for San Francisco and New York City reaching record levels of residents. Of all central cities with now-fixed city limits that reversed population decline, only Atlanta, Denver, Richmond, Seattle, and Washington, D.C., added White residents.

Yet the few thousands of new White residents of Atlanta, Denver, Richmond, and Seattle added *zero* children to their cities' public schools. These residents either had no children or sent them to private schools.

In fact, across metropolitan America, the "melting pot" of our public school system was developing cracks. Segregation of Black pupils continued to diminish slowly, except where an increasingly conservative federal judiciary dismantled long-standing school desegregation orders. (Returning Black children to their neighborhood schools meant sending them back to racially segregated schools.) Segregation of Hispanic and Asian pupils, however, grew wherever a major influx of new immigrants occurred. In most regions, economic segregation—the separation of low-income pupils from middle-class pupils—increased.

Why is this important? The principal reason is that by far the two most important predictors of academic success or failure are (a) the income and educational attainment of a child's parents and (b) the same factors for the parents of a child's classmates. The socioeconomic status of the kids in the classroom is much more important than expenditures per pupil, class size, teacher experience, instructional materials, or competition from charter or private schools that are the typical targets of school reformers. As sociologist James Coleman wrote in his landmark *Equality of Educational Opportunity* (1966), "The educational resources provided by a child's fellow students are more important for his achievement than are the resources provided by the school board." So important are fellow students, Coleman found, that "the social composition of the student body is more highly related to achievement, independent of the student's own social background, than is any school factor."[2]

Summarizing the enormous body of research, the Century Foundation's Richard D. Kahlenberg writes:

> What makes a school good or bad is not so much the physical plant and facilities as the people involved in it—the students, the parents, and the teachers. The portrait of the nation's high poverty schools is not just a racist or classist stereotype: high-poverty schools are often marked by students who have less motivation and are often subject to negative peer influences; parents who are generally less active, exert less clout in school affairs, and garner fewer financial resources for the school; and teachers who tend to be less qualified, to have lower expectations, and to teach a watered-down curriculum. Giving all students access to schools with a core of middle-class students and parents will significantly raise the overall quality of schooling in America.

Coleman's study and those of scores of others can be summarized in two findings:

- *Finding 1:* The socioeconomic status of pupils and classmates largely determines academic outcomes.
- *Finding 2:* Poor children learn best surrounded by middle-class classmates.

In recent years, these findings have been consistently—I would say even deliberately—ignored by almost all politicians and many educators. Politicians and educators refuse to discuss (much less deal with) the racial and class substructure of American society *because too many benefit from maintaining such divisions*. Yet economic integration works. Mixing poor children into predominantly middle-class classrooms would be the most effective way to raise performance levels (revisit Box 2.5).

This is why, in my view, the nature of the rebound of a number of inelastic cities in the 1990s and 2000s signals something unsettling. We are creating "enclave cities," where islands of higher-income, childless, largely White professional households are sealed off from declining neighborhoods of ever poorer, mostly minority families (revisit Box 2.3). Meanwhile, many Black and Hispanic middle-class families are themselves moving to closer-in suburbs only to find that many young, White middle-class families have already decamped to the outer suburbs, taking better jobs, better shopping, and the best schools with them.

As Mayor William Johnson of Rochester, New York, reflecting on his decades as an Urban League executive, said, "We prepared ourselves for opportunity without realizing that opportunity was being relentlessly relocated beyond our reach."

Thirty-five years ago I raised these themes—suburban sprawl; urban disinvestment; racial, ethnic, and economic segregation, all compounded by jurisdictional fragmentation—at the U.S. Conference of Mayors. I got virtually no support. Suburban mayors did not want to think about central cities. They believed their constituents had said good-bye and good riddance to the city. Central city mayors—more and more, Black or Hispanic—did not want to hear any proposals that might threaten their political comfort levels. After all, Black and Hispanic communities had worked long and hard to get real power at city hall.

City and suburban mayors alike were unwilling to attack the urban problem as a matter of racial and economic segregation. From the then-suburban perspective, the strategy was to quarantine "them" in inner-city ghettos and barrios away from "us" and (maybe) help "them" build from within with more federal and state money. For many central city mayors, "them" was "us"—the political base of their power. "Just empower us," they said, "and we'll do the job of fighting urban poverty." ("Empower" typically meant send more federal and state money.) Both suburban and city officials implicitly believed that separate could be made equal—or at least equal enough to be tolerable.

"Separate but equal" cannot work. It has never worked. Ghettos and barrios create and perpetuate an urban underclass. *Bad communities defeat good programs.* Successful clients of social programs typically move away. In inner cities, individual success rarely translates into community success. Life in ghettos and barrios gets worse. Despite flourishing downtowns, most inner-city neighborhoods deteriorate as places to raise families. With shrinking tax bases, city budgets are unable to meet rising social needs.

Enterprise zones, community development banks, nonprofit inner-city housing developers—all tools of "empowerment"—are not futile efforts. They produce some new businesses, some new jobs, some new homes, and some revitalized neighborhoods. They are more effective, however, if carried out within a framework of actions to bring down the walls between city and suburb.

National urban policy, state-by-state urban policy, and area-by-area urban policy must focus on breaking up ghettos and barrios. Urban policy must systematically help ghetto and barrio residents become integrated into the entire metropolitan area. It is the very isolation and hyperconcentration of poor minorities that overwhelms them individually. Neither poor people nor inner cities can succeed if they are cast into the sociological equivalents of giant public housing projects.

Throughout history, cities have been the arena of opportunity and upward mobility. In America the "city" has been redefined since World War II. The real city is now the whole urban area—city and suburb—the metropolitan area. Redeeming inner cities and the urban underclass requires reintegration of city and suburb.

But cities must not become more balanced at the cost of resegregating First Suburbs. To stabilize increasingly racially and economi-

---

Box 4.1 Building ONE America Organizes First Suburbs

On a humid July day in 2011, more than 170 mayors, township supervisors, county commissioners, school board members, and superintendents from older suburbs in 22 metro areas packed a White House auditorium for the White House Forum on First Suburbs, Inclusion, Sustainability, and Economic Growth.

At the White House's invitation, the event was organized by Building ONE America (BOA), a national grassroots–grass-tops movement to organize America's older suburbs to champion basic reforms in state and federal policies affecting their communities.

Participants heard talks on Obama administration policies by Ray LaHood, secretary of the U.S. Department of Transportation, and Pete Rouse, counselor to the president, as well as presentations from BOA's three national strategic partners: Professor john powell (Ohio State's Kirwan Institute for the Study of Race and Ethnicity), Professor Myron Orfield (University of Minnesota's Institute on Race and Poverty), and David Rusk (Innovative Housing Institute).

Afterward, a smaller group met with White House staff in the West Wing while Mike Kruglik, BOA's executive director, briefed President Obama in the Oval Office.[a]

BOA was formed in winter–spring 2009, when three of the most successful grassroots organizing coalitions (the New Jersey Regional Coalition, the Baltimore Regional Initiative Developing Genuine Equality, and the Southeastern Pennsylvania First Sub-

cally diverse, now-inclusive inner suburbs, the still-exclusive outer suburbs need to do their fair share. That will not happen voluntarily in most outer suburbs (see Box 4.1).

This is the toughest political issue in American society. It goes right to the heart of Americans' fears about race and class. There will be no short-term, politically comfortable solutions.

How metro areas are organized has greatly affected the degree of racial and economic segregation. Within their expanding municipal boundaries, elastic Big Box cities capture much suburban-style growth. As the urban core expands, much wealth still remains within the Big Box; elastic cities minimize city–suburb disparities. In addition, neighborhood by neighborhood, different racial, ethnic, and economic groups mix together more readily within a Big Box than they do among many little boxes. Little boxes regions function to divide rather than unify.

---

urbs Project) joined with BOA's three national strategic partners and the Washington-based Poverty and Race Research Action Council. Subsequent organizing efforts have targeted several additional states, including Connecticut, Ohio, Michigan, Illinois, Colorado, and Arizona.

In September 2009, BOA sponsored Building ONE America: A National Summit on Regional Opportunity. The summit convened more than 425 delegates from 18 states to hear from administration and congressional leadership and to press forward its reform agenda. A half-dozen statewide summits have subsequently been held.

Changing the rules of the game at state and federal levels requires bringing together the voting power of First Suburbs and central cities, but the cities themselves have many long-established champions. Though city and First Suburb interests often coincide, BOA's groups currently focus on organizing suburban communities without direct city involvement. "Too often, particularly in meetings with federal officials," one veteran BOA organizer has observed, "having the big-city mayor at the table sucks all the air out of the room. First Suburbs need to speak with their own independent and distinctive voice."

a. Kruglik was one of Barack Obama's two direct supervisors when young Obama was a community organizer in Chicago for three and one-half years.

How can responsibility for poor minorities be made a metropolitan-wide responsibility? How can all jurisdictions—city and suburb—assume their fair share?

Traditionally, the primary purpose of regional cooperation among local governments has been the delivery of public services. Regional arrangements usually avoid policies and programs that share the social burdens of inner-city residents. Yet this is the heart of the challenge. Area-wide compacts on transportation planning, solid waste management, sewage treatment, and air quality management may be good government, but they do not address the urban problem—racial and economic segregation.

For many small and medium-sized metro areas, the best framework for reversing patterns of racial and economic segregation is to create metro governments. This can be achieved by expanding the central city through aggressive annexation policies, by consolidating the city and county, or by fully empowering county government and abolishing or reducing the role of municipalities in key regional issues such as land use and transportation planning, mixed-income housing policy, and economic development.

For larger, more complex metro areas, metro governments may be neither politically feasible nor administratively desirable for delivering services. Larger government is not necessarily more efficient government. At any scale, efficiency is largely a function of good management. Given the bureaucratic impulse of many large systems, a metro government may be less efficient and less responsive as a deliverer of services than smaller governments.

It is not important that local residents have their garbage picked up by a metro-wide garbage service or their parks managed by a metro-wide parks and recreation department. It is important that all local governments pursue common policies that will diminish racial and economic segregation. The following three policies are essential:

- To diminish racial and economic segregation and eliminate concentrated poverty, implement regional inclusionary zoning and other mixed-income housing strategies for integrating low-income households into middle-class communities (see Box 3.1).
- To control suburban sprawl and reverse urban disinvestment, implement regional land use and transportation planning and growth management strategies (see Box 3.2).
- To reduce fiscal imbalances that result from uneven growth and socioeconomic imbalances, implement regional tax-base sharing between richer and poorer jurisdictions (see Box 3.3).

State government must play the leading role. Local government is the creature of state government. State government sets the ground rules for how local governments are organized and what they are empowered to do. Furthermore, governors and state legislators can and do act as metro-wide policy makers. State government also plays an increasingly important role in financing local government (especially, public schools). With the purse comes additional power and responsibility to make the organization of metro areas more rational and equitable.

State government must act in two directions. First, it must build metropolitan institutions by

- Improving annexation laws to facilitate continuous central city expansion into urbanizing areas
- Enacting laws to encourage city–county consolidation or mandating consolidation by direct statute
- Empowering county governments in highly balkanized little boxes states so that they can act as metro governments in key policy and service areas

Second, it must set new rules of the game by

- Requiring all local governments in metro areas to provide fair-share affordable housing, including by adopting local inclusionary zoning ordinances
- Enacting strong, anti-sprawl, statewide growth management laws
- Establishing metro-wide tax base sharing arrangements or using state aid to help equalize local revenues

As I stated earlier, reorganizing local government is primarily a state and local task. The federal government has key roles, however. Since World War II, the federal government's "urban policy" has been "suburban policy." It is past time for the federal government to deal with the consequences of its handiwork through penalizing rather than rewarding sprawl through its infrastructure grants, strengthening the scope of metropolitan planning organization, and promoting mixed-income housing through its various housing finance mechanisms.

Over 80 percent of all minorities now live in America's metropolitan areas. A racially equitable society can be achieved only if urban America is changed. Conversely, solving the problems of cities requires addressing the city–suburb schisms that have intensified since World War II.

More than increased urban aid or even a true "urban policy," what is most needed is a commitment to a spirit of shared sacrifice and renewal. We must exchange the old politics of exclusion for a new politics of inclusion. Solving our "urban problem" will test whether the American people can develop a new spirit of community. Can we truly become *E pluribus unum*—from the many, one?

Notes

1.   These 21 cities are (in descending order of size) Chicago, Philadelphia, Oakland, Minneapolis, Newark, Jersey City, Norfolk, Richmond, Grand Rapids, Worcester, Providence, Springfield (Massachusetts), Paterson, Bridgeport, New Haven, Hartford, Allentown, Albany, Reading, Wilmington (Delaware), and Harrisburg. In addition, growth in Hispanic population accounted for 91 percent of Davenport's population rebound and 99 percent of Salt Lake City's.

2.   Quoted in Richard D. Kahlenberg, *All Together Now: Creating Middle-Class Schools through Public School Choice* (Washington, DC: Brookings Institution Press, 2001), 28, and subsequent quote, 47. Kahlenberg's 33 pages of footnotes to Chapters 3 and 4 catalogue most of the major studies that have been done on the effects of racial and economic integration of the public schools.

Appendix A

Successful City–County Consolidations

Year	City	County	State	Try on which accomplished
1805	New Orleans	Orleans Parish	Louisiana	n.a.
1821	Boston	Suffolk County	Massachusetts	n.a.
1821	Nantucket Town	Nantucket County	Massachusetts	n.a.
1854	Philadelphia	Philadelphia County	Massachusetts	n.a.
1856	San Francisco	San Francisco County	California	n.a.
1897	New York City	Bronx, Kings, New York, Queens, and Richmond Counties	New York	n.a.
1902	Denver	Denver County	Colorado	n.a.
1947	Baton Rouge	East Baton Rouge Parish	Louisiana	1st
1952	Hampton and Phoebus	Elizabeth City County	Virginia	2nd
1957	Newport News	Warwick County	Virginia	2nd
1962	Nashville	Davidson County	Tennessee	2nd
1962	South Norfolk (Chesapeake)	Norfolk County	Virginia	1st
1962	Virginia Beach	Princess Anne County	Virginia	1st
1967	Jacksonville	Duval County	Florida	2nd
1969	Carson City	Ormsby County	Nevada	1st
1969	Indianapolis	Marion County	Indiana	—[a]

Year	City	County	State	Try on which accomplished
1970	Columbus	Muscogee County	Georgia	2nd
1970	Juneau	Greater Juneau Borough	Alaska	1st
1971	Holland and Whaleyville	Nansemond County	Virginia	1st
1971	Sitka	Greater Sitka Borough	Alaska	1st
1972	Lexington	Fayette County	Kentucky	1st
1972	Suffolk	Nansemond City-County	Virginia	1st
1975	Anchorage	Greater Anchorage Borough	Alaska	3rd
1976	Anaconda	Deer Lodge County	Montana	1st
1976	Butte	Silver Bow County	Montana	2nd
1981	Houma	Terrebonne Parrish	Louisiana	1st
1988	Lynchburg City	Moore County	Tennessee	1st
1990	Athens	Clarke County	Georgia	4th
1992	Lafayette	Lafayette Parish	Louisiana	1st
1992	Yakutat	Yakuta Borough	Alaska	1st
1995	Augusta	Richmond County	Georgia	5th
1997	Kansas City	Wyandotte County	Kansas	1st
2000	Hartsville	Trousdale County	Tennessee	1st
2000	Louisville	Jefferson County	Kentucky	3rd
2002	Haines	Haines Borough	Alaska	2nd
2003	Cusseta	Chattahoochee County	Georgia	1st
2006	Georgetown	Quitman County	Georgia	1st
2007	Tribune	Greeley County	Kansas	1st
2008	Preston	Webster County	Georgia	1st
2008	Satenville	Echols County	Georgia	1st

Sources: Web page of Chris Briem: http://www.briem.com/frag/CityCountyReferenda .htm; Suzanne M. Leland and Kurt Thurmaier, eds., *Case Studies in City–County Consolidation* (Washington, DC: Georgetown University Press, 2004); "City–County Consolidation Proposals," National Association of Counties, Washington, DC, http:// www.naco.org/counties/documents/city%20county%20consolidations.01.01.2011.pdf.
Note: n.a. = not applicable.
a. Consolidation did not require referendum.

Appendix B

Potential City–County Consolidations

The 27 "best bet" communities (shown in Table B.1) for city–county consolidation share common characteristics:

- All central cities contain at least 60 percent of their county's population. Generally, in successful consolidation referenda, a larger number of pro-consolidation city voters are necessary to outweigh a smaller number of anti-consolidation county voters, including both those living in smaller municipalities and those living in unincorporated areas.
- All 12 states have authorized city–county mergers.
- Since World War II, successful city–county consolidations have taken place already in Georgia (seven), Tennessee (three), Louisiana (three), Kansas (two), Montana (two), Florida, Indiana, and Colorado.[1] These successes improve the odds of further city–county consolidations being approved in these states (but hardly guarantee it).

In some instances, an effort to launch formal city–county consolidation might generate more political heat than success would ultimately be worth. Charlotte, for example, continues to implement a very successful annexation program, adding 55 square miles, or 23 percent, to its city limits of 298 square miles in the past decade. Between Charlotte's 80 percent share of Mecklenburg County's population and the 15 percent share of its six suburban municipalities, only 5 percent of the county's people live on unincorporated land (though the unincorporated area still represents 100 square miles of the county's 527 square miles). Moreover, city and county governments have a close working partnership; one or the other provides county-wide services (e.g., Charlotte provides police protection for both the city and unincorporated county, while Mecklenburg County handles all parks and recreation programs). Most notably, city and county have a single planning department and a jointly appointed planning commission.

Thus, the actual circumstances of each potential city–county consolidation must be examined carefully. However, for these 27 best bet prospects, both state law and demographics suggest that a city–county merger is feasible. Moreover, all are Big Box states without townships (with the exception of Indiana, a very soft township state). As a consequence, assuming that smaller municipalities would be explicitly exempted from a proposed merger, no subcounty units of government (such as townships) would resist the merger institutionally.

Nonetheless, voters in 12 of these communities have rejected past merger proposals.[2] A policy of continuing piecemeal annexations may be the realistic path to maintaining the city's elasticity as the region grows. In fact, during the past decade, 24 of the 27 cities successfully added an average of almost 20 percent to their territory through annexation.

In the next category are 42 communities where consolidation is conceivable. Though the minimum electoral demographics are met (i.e., the city is 60 percent or more of the county's population), neither a history of other successful consolidations in the state nor state authorizing laws on the books (with the sole exception of West Virginia) favor consolidation. Of the 42 cities, 36 did successfully annex land in the past decade, adding an average of 10 percent to their municipal territory. However, because the trend is for state legislatures to make annexation more difficult (particularly in Texas), now might be the right time for these communities to explore formal city–county mergers.

In the final group are seven communities in Illinois, Minnesota, Ohio, and Wisconsin for which city–county consolidation is improbable but at least worth examining. Though all are located in semi-soft township states, townships are not constituted as municipalities immunized against annexation. As a consequence, in the past decade, six of these seven cities (Peoria, Illinois; Columbus, Ohio; Eau Claire and Rochester, Minnesota; and Mankato and Kenosha, Wisconsin) successfully added township land to their cities, averaging 15 percent growth. This suggests that, state legislatures permitting, a successful city–county merger would indeed bring a sizable "dowry" to the marriage.

These listings in Appendix B cover only 76 of 383 central cities of U.S. metro areas. Other possibilities involving secondary central cities in metro areas (e.g., St. Petersburg–Pinellas County, Florida, or Council Bluffs–Pottawattomie County, Iowa) have not been analyzed.

Finally, the following is important to reemphasize:

- City–county consolidation is irrelevant in hard township states (the six states of New England, Pennsylvania, New York, and New Jersey). Beyond any consideration of political feasibility, no likelihood whatsoever exists that any independent borough or village, town or township, or smaller city would merge with the central city and county governments; thus, no dowry is available for the central city in such a marriage.

- Experience shows that, unless the city represents at least 60 percent of the county's voters, no realistic prospect exists that a merger will be approved except in the rarest of circumstances (such as Louisville–Jefferson County). Thus, though I have analyzed all other central cities–central counties in the remaining 307 metro areas, they are not represented in Appendix B.

Notes

1. In Colorado's case, Denver (1900) and Bloomfield (2001) created new county governments within the boundaries of existing cities; there have been no "conventional" city–county consolidations. These two consolidations are more akin to Virginia's system of independent cities that combine both municipal and county functions.

2. In fact, Albuquerque and Tallahassee are four-time losers.

Table B.1
Potential City–County Consolidations, Based on Census 2010

Central city	Central county	State	City as percentage of county population	Unincorporated area as percentage of county population	Number of suburban municipalities in county	Suburban municipalities as percentage of county population	General state law authorizing consolidation	Failed consolidation referenda	Number of other post–World War II consolidations in state	Increase in city area through annexation, 2000–2010
Category 1: Best bets—consolidation feasible (27 cities)										21
Durham	Durham	NC	85	14	3	1	Yes	1961, 1974	0	13
Albuquerque	Bernalillo	NM	82	17	4	1	Yes	1959, 1973, 2003, 2004	0	4
Albany	Dougherty	GA	82	18	0	0	Yes	1954, 1956	7	0
Charlotte	Mecklenburg	NC	80	5	6	15	Yes	1971	0	23
Portland	Multnomah	OR	79	2	8	18	Yes	1927, 1974	0	0
Lawrence	Douglas	KS	79	11	3	10	Yes		2	19
Palm Coast	Flagler	FL	79	14	4	7	Yes		1	77
Shreveport	Caddo Parish	LA	78	17	10	5	Yes		3	2
Clarksville	Montgomery	TN	77	23	0	–1	Yes	1981, 1996	3	3
Wichita	Sedgwick	KS	77	7	19	16	Yes		2	17
Manhattan	Riley	KS	74	21	4	5	Yes		2	25
Great Falls	Cascade	MT	72	26	3	2	Yes		2	12
Topeka	Shawnee	KS	72	26	4	2	Yes	2005	2	7
Fort Wayne	Allen	IN	71	21	7	8	Yes		1	40
Billings	Yellowstone	MT	70	25	2	4	Yes		2	29
Memphis	Shelby	TN	70	17	6	13	Yes	1962, 1971, 2010	3	13
Yuba City	Sutter	CA	69	23	1	8	Yes		0	56

City	County	State								
Colorado Springs	El Paso	CO	67	27	7	6	No		0	5
Pueblo	Pueblo	CO	67	33	2	0	No		0	19
Jackson	Madison	TN	66	32	3	2	Yes	1987	3	0
Tallahassee	Leon	FL	66	34	0	0	Yes	1971, 1973, 1976, 1992	1	5
Winston-Salem	Forsyth	NC	65	14	9	21	Yes		0	22
Evansville	Vanderburgh	IN	65	34	1	1	Yes	1974	1	8
Corvallis	Benton	OR	64	22	4	14	Yes		0	4
Fayetteville	Cumberland	NC	63	28	7	9	Yes		0	148
Missoula	Missoula	MT	61	39	0	0	Yes	1975, 1983	2	16
Muncie	Delaware	IN	60	26	7	14	Yes		1	12
Category 2: Consolidation conceivable (42 cities)										**9**
Laredo	Webb	TX	94	2	2	4	No		0	13
Lincoln	Lancaster	NE	91	7	12	2	No		0	19
Amarillo	Potter	TX	90	10	1	0	No		0	11
Montgomery	Montgomery	AL	90	8	1	2	No		0	3
Corpus Christi	Nueces	TX	90	4	10	6	No		0	4
St. Joseph	Buchanan	MO	86	12	7	1	No		0	0
Abilene	Taylor	TX	85	11	7	4	No		0	2
San Angelo	Tom Green	TX	85	15	0	0	No		0	2
Lubbock	Lubbock	TX	82	11	8	6	No		0	7

Table B.1
Potential City–County Consolidations, Based on Census 2010 (continued)

Central city	Central county	State	City as percentage of county population	Unincorporated area as percentage of county population	Number of suburban municipalities in county	Suburban municipalities as percentage of county population	General state law authorizing consolidation	Failed consolidation referenda	Number of other post–World War II consolidations in state	Increase in city area through annexation, 2000–2010
Lewiston	Nez Perce	ID	81	14	3	5	No		0	4
Midland	Midland	TX	81	18	1	1	No		0	8
El Paso	El Paso	TX	81	12	5	7	No		0	2
Sioux City	Woodbury	IA	81	8	14	11	No		0	5
Wichita Falls	Wichita	TX	80	3	5	17	No		0	2
Omaha	Douglas	NE	79	19	6	2	No		0	10
Grand Forks	Grand Forks	ND	79	15	9	6	No		0	4
Lawton	Comanche	OK	78	14	9	8	No		0	8
San Antonio	Bexar	TX	77	15	25	8	No		0	13
Austin	Travis	TX	76	16	18	8	No		0	18
Bismarck	Burleigh	ND	75	21	4	4	No		0	15
Casper	Natrona	WY	73	15	5	12	No		0	12
Odessa	Ector	TX	73	27	1	0	No		0	14
Victoria	Victoria	TX	72	28	0	0	No		0	8
Sioux Falls	Minnehaha	SD	72	16	10	12	No		0	30
Jackson	Hinds	MS	71	17	7	12	No		0	6
Fargo	Cass	ND	70	4	26	26	No		0	29
Jonesboro	Craighead	AR	70	19	9	11	No		0	0
Oklahoma City	Oklahoma	OK	69	0	19	31	No		0	0

City	County	State							
Fort Smith	Sebastian	AR	69	14	10	17	No	0	23
Rapid City	Pennington	SD	67	22	7	11	No	0	24
Columbia	Boone	MO	67	27	8	6	No	0	19
Ames	Story	IA	66	10	14	24	No	0	12
Pocatello	Bannock	ID	65	13	6	22	No	0	14
Longview	Gregg	TX	65	16	7	19	No	0	2
Cheyenne	Laramie	WY	65	33	3	2	No	0	16
Dothan	Houston	AL	64	21	11	14	No	0	3
Wheeling	Ohio	WV	64	16	5	20	Yes	0	0
Tulsa	Tulsa	OK	64	8	12	28	No	0	8
Pine Bluff	Jefferson	AR	63	32	6	5	No	0	0
Dubuque	Dubuque	IA	62	20	20	18	No	0	13
Davenport	Scott	IA	60	9	16	30	No	0	0
Cedar Rapids	Linn	IA	60	10	17	30	No	0	12
Category 3: Consolidation improbable (7 cities)									13
Rochester	Olmsted	MN	74	15	7	11	Yes	0	38
Decatur	Macon	IL	69	13	11	18	No	0	0
Columbus	Franklin	OH	67	8	26	25	Yes	0	6
Eau Claire	Eau Claire	WI	65	25	4	10	No	0	6
Peoria	Peoria	IL	62	20	15	18	No	0	8
Mankato	Blue Earth	MN	61	22	12	17	Yes	0	18
Kenosha	Kenosha	WI	60	22	5	19	No	0	13

Sources

All data not otherwise indicated are taken from either publications or the website of the Bureau of the Census of the U.S. Department of Commerce (http://www.census.gov). These data cover the decennial censuses from 1950 to 2010 as well as the American Community Survey 2005–09, the annual *Statistical Abstract of the United States,* and the U.S. Gazetteer for 2000 and 2010.

Metropolitan racial segregation indices for both housing markets and elementary schools were originally provided by the Lewis Mumford Center for Comparative Urban and Regional Research of the State University of New York at Albany. That archive is now located at the American Communities Project at Brown University (http://www.s4.brown.edu/S4/Projects_ACP.htm). Economic segregation indices for 1969 to 2009 are available from the same source.

All information on metro area employment trends comes from the Regional Economic Accounts of the Bureau of Economic Analysis of the U.S. Department of Commerce (http://www.bea.gov/iTable/iTable.cfm?ReqID=70&step=1&isuri=1&acrdn=5) for the periods 1969–2000 (SAIS) and 2001 forward (NAICS).

The source for municipal bond ratings is the October 2002 edition of the Mergent Bond Record (http://www.mergent.com) for ratings provided by Moody's Investors Service. They have been updated since through the Moody's website at http://www.moodys .com/researchandratings/market-segment/u.s.-public-finance/city -(incl.-town-village-and-township)/005003004001/4294966088%20 4294961994/4294967230/0/0/-/0/-/-/-/-/-/-/-/en/global/pdf/rra.

The analysis of state laws regarding city–county consolidation, municipal formation, and annexation powers is adapted from *State Laws Governing Local Government Structure and Administration* (Washington, DC: U.S. Advisory Commission on Intergovernmental Relations, March 1993). Table 1.6 is adapted from an earlier study by Melvin B. Hill Jr., *State Laws Governing Local Government Structure and Administration* (Athens, GA: Institute of Government, University of Georgia, 1971).

Finally, readers with questions or seeking information may contact me by phone (202/364-2455) or by e-mail (davidrusk@verizon.net). E-mail is best because I have lost my hearing in recent years and hear with the aid of a cochlear implant (a miraculous technology, but I may have to beg telephone callers' patience at times).

Index

Note: The notations n and *t* after page numbers refer to notes and tables respectively.

civil rights: grassroot organizations,
162; growth patterns, 32; housing
rights, 33; little boxes planning
and zoning, 52
Civil Rights Act of 1968, 33
Cleveland: boundaries, 22–23; contribute effect, 34; deindustrialization,
55, 57; economic development,
102–3; elasticity, 76; household
decline, 37, 82; income, 47, 58;
lack of elbow room, 25; paired
with Columbus, 4, 14; population
growth, 19; population loss, 34;
racial segregation, 46, 67n12
Colorado, city–county consolidations,
179, 181n1
Columbus: capture effect, 34; deindustrialization, 57; elasticity, 76;
elbow room, 25; new-home occupants, 14; paired with Cleveland,
4, 14; population growth, 19, 34,
37; racial segregation, 67n12;
school districts, 53
community development banks, 171
community leaders, 102–3, 162
Community Reinvestment Act, 33, 157
competitiveness, economic, 101–3
composite elasticity profile, 61–63
composite elasticity score, 71
Connecticut: affordable housing,
146–47
consolidation: cities without suburbs,
111–18; city–county, 17, 18–19,
22, 23, 25, 133–41, 175, 177–81,
182t–85t; municipal enclaves, 127,
135–36; New York City, 12–13,
135, 137; school district, 163n2
consolidation charter commissions,
138
constituency, sense of, 52, 95
Corpus Christi, Hispanic population,
85
cost of living, 105, 106t, 118, 121n21
county governments, 147–48; empowering, 147–48, 175; functions,
147; history, 147; unincorporated
land, 127
county states, 131–33
creative class cluster, 97, 98–99
Creativity Index, 98–99

debt management, 59–61

declining cities, 105–11, 108t–9t;
Chicago comeback, 107–10; criteria, 105–7; loss of households,
108t–9t, 110–11
deindustrialization: Charlotte, 2, 6n5;
Frost Belt–Sun Belt, 56–57, 101;
Grand Rapids, 2, 6n5; labor market effects, 55–57, 56t; regional
patterns, 97–101, 100t
desegregation plans, 53–55, 94–95,
169
Detroit: auto industry, 101; boundaries, 22–23; contribute effect, 34;
deindustrialization, 55; economic
development, 102–3; elasticity,
76; household decline, 37, 82;
income, 47; lack of elbow room,
25; paired with Houston, 4, 14;
population loss, 34, 37; racial
segregation, 42–43, 46, 67n12
diffusion, 91t, 92–96, 102–3
discrimination in housing, federal
programs, 32–33
discriminatory public policies, urban
growth related, 31–34

economic development: city-suburbs
related, 95–97; competitiveness,
101–3; creative class, 97, 98–99;
diffusion related, 92–94; job
creation rates, 103, 104t; private–
public partnership, 102–3
economic segregation: Atlanta, 80–81;
calculating, 67n13; diminishing,
regions of, 120n16; elasticity
scores compared, 87–91, 88t,
89t; federal policy, 153–59; racial
segregation, 3, 46–47, 46t; rules
of the game, 3; school district,
169–70
edge cities, 95
educational levels, workforce, 61, 62t,
67n17
elastic cities: age of, 27–30, 27t, 90, 90t;
annexation, 11, 21–25; capture
of suburban growth, 34–36, 35t,
78, 79t; composite profile, 61–63;
elasticity score, 71–73, 74t–75t;
household size, 37–39, 40t, 82–83,
83t; new-home occupants, 14–17,
15t; population growth, 11–17,
36–37, 36t, 76, 77t; poverty, 47–50